MW00414625

How to Live an Extraordinary Life

Anthony Pompliano writes 65 letters to his children with inspiring lessons on how to succeed in business, have great relationships, do well with money, and live a healthier and happier life.

What does it take to make the most of what really matters (and to know what that is before it passes you by)? To overcome obstacles that set most people back (and to see them coming beforehand)? To flourish not just financially—but also in your family, free time, and the world of business?

What does it take to live an extraordinary life?

The answers will surprise you.

Anthony Pompliano has lived in a war zone, met and interviewed the world's wealthiest people, built and sold companies, invested in more than 200 businesses, formed friendships around the globe, started a loving family, and found happiness. Along the way, he has kept a personal list of the lessons he has learned.

Now, in *How to Live an Extraordinary Life*, he writes 65 letters to his children laying out each lesson and how he learned it, and explaining how it can be applied by anyone in their life today.

The result is a compelling collection of practical and inspiring life strategies that anyone can use to build an extraordinary life.

You will find unique advice about using your childhood as a chisel, understanding that luck is not real, living your life as a documentary, developing unshakable resilience, becoming a happier person, and much, much more.

Most importantly, Anthony shows that an extraordinary life is within reach for anyone who wants it. You can start right now.

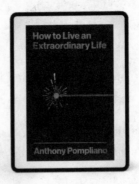

How to Live an Extraordinary Life

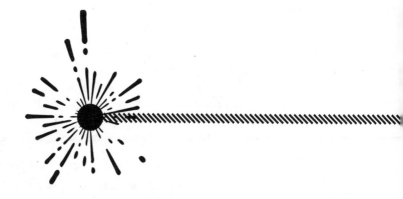

Anthony Pompliano

Harriman House

Harriman House Ltd
3 Viceroy Court
Bedford Road
Petersfield
Hampshire
GU32 3LJ
GREAT BRITAIN
Tel: +44 (0)1730 233870

Email: enquiries@harriman-house.com
Website: harriman.house

First published in 2024.

Hardback ISBN: 978-0-85719-992-8
Paperback ISBN: 978-1-80409-108-1
eBook ISBN: 978-0-85719-993-5

British Library Cataloguing in Publication Data

A CIP catalogue record for this book can be obtained from the British Library.

To Polina, life with you is extraordinary

Contents

Contents

Introduction

I never thought I would see my 35th birthday. When I was younger and friends would ask me what I wanted to be when I grew up, I always caveated the answer with, "Well, I am going to die before 35 so I have to accomplish my goals before then."

I am not sure why I thought this way.

It could have been because I was always doing reckless things as a teenager. There were multiple car accidents and fist fights. I went to war in Iraq as part of the US Army when I was 20 years old. I was fond of driving my motorcycle over 100 mph in my early 20s. And I drank and partied even more than your average young man.

To be honest, I had an incredible time. I don't regret a single second of it. But I figured you couldn't live life that fast and expect to make it past age 35.

I was wrong.

I am writing this book a few months after I turned 35 years old. Every day I get from here until the end of my life is borrowed time in my mind. This milestone made me reflect on everything I have packed into the last 35 years.

My life has allowed me to visit more than 30 countries, meet many of the world's most successful people, build a family I love, help thousands of people improve their lives, and achieve financial independence.

Simply, I have lived an extraordinary life.

You won't find me riding a motorcycle these days, nor will you see me partying or going off to war. Those days are long gone. Today, I have an amazing wife and two young kids who I cherish.

As I reflected on where I was before, where I am today, and where I would like to go in the future, I was compelled to write a letter to each of my children about the things I have learned so far. Two letters turned into five letters. Five letters turned into ten. And next thing I knew, I had written more than 60 letters to my son and daughter.

This book is a collection of those letters. Each chapter contains a lesson about something that I learned in my life. These lessons can stand on their own, or they can be combined with other lessons in the book. Sometimes these lessons complement each other and other times the lessons may contradict each other.

Context matters when you are sharing advice, so evaluate each lesson independently.

Before we get started, I also want to leave a message to the many people that have known me over the years. Most of you know me as an entrepreneur, an investor, or someone with a large social media following.

I am proud of everything I have accomplished in my professional life, but the most important thing to me is ensuring that my children are prepared to be happy, productive citizens in the world.

These letters were started out of fear that something could happen to me before I had the chance to share these stories and this advice with my kids. I guess it was a resurfacing of that old feeling that I wouldn't make it past 35.

But then, as the letters accumulated, they became something that I thought would be useful for a much wider audience. And so the book was created out of hope that these letters could help even more people around the world.

The funny thing about writing a book like this is that people start thinking I must believe I have all the answers. That couldn't be further from the truth. In fact, I am hyper-aware of how much more I have to learn.

Hopefully the book I write in the next 35 years will be three times longer and full of even more lessons.

Anthony

How you do anything is how you do everything

Sofia & Leo,

Everything in your life is made up of details.

From the work you pursue to the relationships you cherish to the reputation you earn, the big things are made up of many small things. It can be easy to forget about the small things though. They aren't the big things. They don't seem important in the grand scheme.

But I have found the opposite to be true in my life—how you do anything is how you will do everything.

When I was deployed to Iraq as part of the US Army Infantry in 2008–2009, we would spend hours patrolling our designated areas. These patrols usually occurred late at night under the cover of darkness. During the night patrols, the wind would cover our team, our trucks, and our weapons in sand from the deserts that surrounded us.

We were exhausted when we got back from a patrol. It was tempting to simply go to sleep. But our leadership team had drilled into us that we were not supposed to go to sleep until we meticulously cleaned our trucks and our weapons from the sand.

Their point was that we need to be prepared for the next mission before we went to sleep. Was it likely that we would have to leave on short notice for the next mission without having time to prepare? No.

But they didn't want to take any chances.

It may surprise you to hear that the leadership team never checked whether we cleaned the trucks or our weapons when we got back. They didn't need to. It was well understood that cleaning your weapon was not an action that you did for yourself, but rather something you did to ensure your weapon worked when needed to help your teammates in the future.

Cleaning your weapon was a selfless act.

The exhausted person who will take the time to meticulously clean their weapon before going to sleep is the same person who will be dependable for the team. They will be on time. They will come prepared for every mission. They will look after their teammates. They won't leave anyone behind. They are the type of person that pays attention to the details.

Remember, how you do anything is how you do everything.

It is important to decide what type of person you want to be. Do you show up on time? Do you keep your promises? Do you always complete the job? Do you pay attention to the details? Do you take care of your team?

Once you decide the type of person you want to be, you can start acting like that person immediately. Think of it as your aspirational self. If you want to be a person that shows up on time, then you make sure you are not only on time, but a few minutes early.

You begin to take pride in the small action of never being late. No one knows you're doing it, but eventually you develop a reputation for always being on time.

Guess what else people start to understand? The person who is always on time is the same person who keeps their promises. This person is a trustworthy, dependable person.

Ask yourself: Who do I aspire to be, and what actions does this person take?

Start small. The small things make up the big things. How you do anything is how you do everything.

Dad

Consistency is incredibly valuable.

Consistency is a superpower.

Excellence breeds excellence.

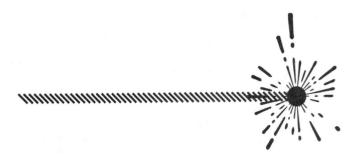

Today is practice for tomorrow

Sofia & Leo,

What you do today is merely practice for tomorrow.

It is easy to forget this lesson. The thing you are working on today seems like the most important thing you have ever worked on. The relationship you are in at the moment feels like the one you will be in forever. And you feel smarter today than you have ever felt in your life.

But do not lose sight of what the future holds.

The first company that I started felt like the one I would work on for the rest of my life. I was building the company with my best friends. The idea and technology was exciting. I didn't have to work for anyone else. We were one day closer to riches with each passing day. Well, at least that is what we thought.

Within one year, it was obvious to me that I would not work on the company for the rest of my life. In fact, I didn't think I could work on it for another six months.

I was in my early 20s and full of enthusiasm. There were so many things I wanted to do. Why would I work on this one idea for the next 40 years? A lot can change in a year.

But building that company wasn't a waste of time. It was actually the foundation of what would become a lifelong passion for entrepreneurship.

My experience building the first company ended up being the perfect practice for building my second company. The second one was bigger, more effective at solving a problem for customers, and ultimately helped me make more money. I don't think I would have been able to build the second company without having worked on the first company for about 18 months.

Once I sold the second company, I took a job running a few product and growth teams at Facebook. I quickly had success inside this fast-growth behemoth. Why? The experience running two companies of my own served as the perfect practice for running high-performance teams at one of the most valuable companies in the world.

Each step in my career followed the same pattern.

I would use one job, company, or product as the stepping stone to the next one. At the time I didn't realize it was practice, but it was always clear in hindsight.

This was not only true in my professional pursuits.

Your mom and I both benefited from dating other people before we met. She wouldn't have liked the younger, immature version of me. I didn't know how to participate in a long-term relationship.

The first girl I ever went on a date with helped me learn how to be a better partner. The second one helped me become more empathetic, kind, and responsible. And that continued until I eventually had the skills and experience that was necessary to care for someone I was deeply in love with.

Every day I am thankful that your mom and I did not meet when I was a teenager or in my early 20s. Our relationship wouldn't have worked because neither of us had enough life experience to know how to build a healthy partnership. I don't know if she would say the same thing from her perspective, but I suspect she believes it is true as well.

Humans are not born with all of the skills, experience, and knowledge necessary to succeed in life. You acquire each of these with time and practice. This phenomenon applies to your work, your relationships, and your hobbies.

Today is practice for tomorrow. Make sure you pay attention to the various lessons you learn. You will need them in the future.

Dad

Watch someone's daily habits today and you will understand what their future looks like.

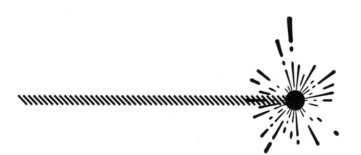

Carve your ethics in stone, write your opinions in sand

Sofia and Leo,

Carve your ethics in stone, but write your opinions in sand.

This is easier said than done.

It requires an immense amount of discipline and maturity. Most people are either unwilling to change their mind at all or they change it way too easily.

That's because most people are intellectually lazy. I recently came across a thought experiment by astrophysicist Neil DeGrasse Tyson in the book, *Hidden Genius*.

Ask yourself this question: If someone tries to sell you crystals that promise to cure all your ailments, what would you do? Believe it outright or reject it immediately?

Tyson says those are both intellectually lazy responses. The best defense against sloppy thinking is skepticism, which requires asking probing questions to get to the root of whether there's supporting proof to back up the claim.

"A proper skeptic questions what they're unsure of but recognizes when valid evidence is presented to change their mind," he says. "It's a path of inquiry toward the truth."

Don't be rigid in your thinking. Understand there are different approaches for different situations. The world is a nuanced place.

That nuance is easily seen in the difference between ethics and opinions.

Ethics are foundational principles that govern how you do things. Never waver on these. Carve them in stone. Always do the right thing.

When faced with questions of ethics, you should make the same decision every time. There is almost nothing that should change throughout your lifetime. Deciphering between right and wrong is an essential skill necessary to navigate the world.

Opinions are different.

These are views you form on what you do. Be willing to change these when the facts change. Write your opinions in sand. Mental flexibility is the name of the game.

If you have the same opinion about every topic throughout your life, you probably aren't learning and growing. You haven't done the work necessary to evaluate your positions. Don't be rigid. Don't marry your ideas.

The balance between ethics and opinions has been tested constantly over the years.

I was once at a conference in Las Vegas. A man approached me and began pitching the idea behind his business. It was obvious that the business was going to make money, but there was one problem— the software product that was being sold was preying on a portion of the population that was economically disadvantaged.

Within the first few minutes of the pitch, it was obvious that I was not going to invest in the company. While it was my opinion that the business would make money, my ethics told me to run as far away from the founder and his organization as possible.

But steering clear of the investment was not good enough. I spent time explaining in excruciating detail why I thought the business and product was unethical. If you carve your ethics in stone, you have to be willing to articulate to others why they may be violating your framework.

But it was one of the easiest decisions I ever made in business.

Never forget—carve your ethics in stone and write your opinions in sand. I wish you the strength to do this daily.

Dad

The smartest people I know:

1. Obsessively read books.

2. Pursue new mental models.

3. Enjoy intelligent discourse.

4. Quickly admit when they're wrong.

5. Are comfortable changing their opinion.

6. Surround themselves with intelligence.

7. Seek to understand every perspective on a topic.

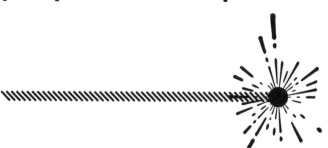

Excellence doesn't have a watch

Sofia & Leo,

An extraordinary life is made by building things of excellence. It can be relationships, companies, investments, or hobby projects.

Excellence rarely happens overnight. The best things in life take time to build.

Think about a skyscraper in New York City. No one shows up one day, snaps their fingers, and creates a building that stretches over 1,000 feet into the air.

Gravity is working against you.

Instead, these buildings are created methodically. Engineering experts spend years architecting the structural plans. Then someone spends months laying a strong foundation that can hold these large, heavy buildings.

Once the foundation is set, the skyscraper is built one floor at a time. It takes hundreds of workers many months to construct these modern marvels.

It is only after all of this work that the world is able to enjoy a physical structure that was previously thought impossible to build.

Excellence takes time.

This is true in all aspects of life.

Take Warren Buffett, one of the world's most successful investors, as another example. He was investing for 40 years before he became a billionaire. That means Buffett worked for four decades to make good decisions, avoid mistakes, and stay patient.

It helps that he had the right strategy, but his company Berkshire Hathaway would not be successful today if Buffett had avoided long-term thinking.

As you are reading this, you may think that construction or investing are not applicable to your life. That may be true.

Let's use an example that is applicable to everyone—health.

If you want to lose weight or gain muscle, it will be nearly impossible to achieve your desired end result if you don't consistently exhibit discipline. Experts claim that the proper speed to lose weight is approximately one pound per week.

So if you want to lose 25 pounds, then you will have to work diligently for nearly six months to achieve your goal. It is not enough to merely do the right thing, which in this case is to eat less calories than you expend, for a short period of time. And then once the weight is off, you can't just go back to your diet from before—you need to continue to eat and live healthily for the rest of your life.

You need to do the right thing for a long period of time.

This concept of time is hard for most people to wrap their head around because we live in a society dominated by short-termism. This is part of human nature as well. Everyone wants things right now. But things that can be created quickly tend to be lower quality.

This means that you can have a competitive advantage in life by having the patience to create high-quality things over long periods of time.

Build a great business. Achieve your fitness goals. Create a happy, loving family. None of these can last unless you apply discipline and patience over many years. There are no shortcuts.

Excellence doesn't have a watch.

Dad

The willingness to eat glass for a decade and keep showing up with the same level of enthusiasm drastically increases your odds of success.

Do it right, do it light

Sofia & Leo,

Extraordinary lives are not devoid of routines.

Humans are creatures of habit. Once a routine or habit is established, we can operate on autopilot for that task.

You don't want to do this for the extraordinary parts of your life, but you do want to make sure a habit ensures you accomplish the mundane, yet important, aspects of your daily life.

Want to always remember to take your multivitamin? Make it a habit. Want to go to the gym every day? Make it a habit. Want to read 25 pages of a book every night before you go to sleep? Make it a habit. Want to ensure you compliment your significant other every morning? Make it a habit.

With a routine, your body and mind don't even need you to think about the things that you have trained them to do automatically.

The logical follow-up question is, "How can I create a habit?"

Bestselling author James Clear breaks down the creation of habits into four simple parts:

1. Cue
2. Craving
3. Response
4. Reward

The cue starts the behavior. The craving motivates you to desire a result. The response is the tiny habit you perform. The reward is what happens *after* you've executed the habit. It's a powerful cycle present in our everyday lives.

The thing I learned from James Clear is that we can program our bodies to execute whatever routine we want as long as we are intentional with our instructions.

Building habits is the best way I have found to create repetition in the actions that I want to do on a daily, weekly, monthly, or annual basis.

You can lie to yourself and say you will remember—you won't. You can bet on an indomitable willpower to accomplish your big, audacious goals—eventually you will succumb to entropy.

Don't try to be a hero in your own story. Create habits that save you from yourself. A few weeks spent building the right habit will pay off for a lifetime.

There is a saying in the Army: "Do it wrong, do it long. Do it right, do it light." Habits are not only right, but they also will make the work light and effortless.

Build good habits.

Dad

Build good habits and consistency will do the rest of the work.

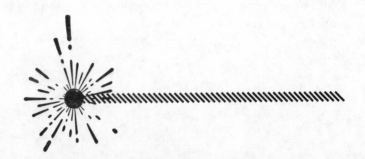

Build things

Sofia & Leo,

You will get the most fulfillment in life from creating value.

Creation requires optimism. You have to see the future world you want to live in and then spend the time, money, and energy to make it a reality.

I could list thousands of things that I have created in my life—from memories to companies—that have left a positive feeling in my head and heart. The two that stand out the most to me are creating our family and helping so many people create companies.

Creating our family is my most cherished accomplishment. Your mother and I spent a lot of time making sure we built the foundation for a great family. We are best friends. We respect each other. We want to see each other succeed. We want to grow old together and live an extraordinary life together.

Part of an extraordinary life, for us, is having children and raising them to be happy, productive members of society.

There were many long nights of conversation about how we wanted to raise our children. What were the values we wanted to teach them? What skills did we feel were essential for them to learn? What type of schooling did we want to pursue? What type of parents did we want to be?

We discussed every possible detail. Most of all, we wanted to raise kids who would be ambitious, independent adults. If we wanted to have a loving family of ambitious people who knew the importance of hard work, then we would have to do the difficult work of raising our children to embrace these ideals.

By no means have we been perfect parents, but your mom and I are proud of the family we have built. We take great joy in seeing each of our children pursue their passions and find success in their chosen interests. *(For now, Sofia's passion is ballet, and Leo's is learning how to crawl.)*

Building a family has been wonderful.

There are a lot of similarities to building a family and building a company. I have played a small role in helping hundreds of companies go from inception to scalable operations. Sometimes I started the company myself. Other times, I contributed capital or made an introduction. Once in a while, I merely provided some advice or encouragement.

These companies have gone on to solve some of the hardest problems in society.

There is Everly Wellness which has pioneered at-home diagnostic testing; Brigit which saves every-day Americans from overdraft fees; Varda which is manufacturing pharmaceutical drugs in space; Eight Sleep which empowers people to get better sleep every night;

and Strike which is helping people buy bitcoin and protect their savings from inflation.

It is incredibly rewarding to spend years working on a business and then stepping back to see what you've created.

There are so many things you can do in your life, but the most fulfilling activity I have ever found is building something. It can be a family, a business, a community, or a hobby. Whatever it is, focus on building something that you value.

The personal enjoyment you get from building something of value far outweighs any financial reward you could ever receive.

Dad

Protect your creativity like your life depends on it.

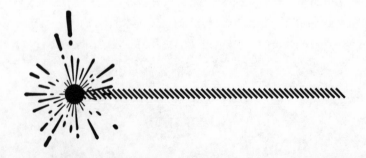

Have a bias for action

Sofia & Leo,

You will stand out in life if you have a bias for action.

The world is filled with people who have grand dreams and audacious plans. They talk about all the amazing things they will accomplish one day. Yet none of it seems to ever come to fruition.

I did not understand this until I started building companies in my early 20s. My second company was struggling, and I had no clue how to turn it around. We were trying different things, but none of it was working.

I couldn't understand what we were doing wrong.

So I went to visit a friend out in San Francisco who had successfully built a very large technology company. Part of me wanted to get away from the business problems for two days and part of me was hoping that my friend would have some good advice.

After I explained the problems we were facing, he asked me one question:

"What are you doing about it?"

As soon as he said those words, I knew where I had been messing up. Instead of focusing on action, I had been trying to think my way out of the problem. I was falling victim to the classic paralysis by analysis.

I headed back home and immediately got to work. Thankfully, after a few iterations, we were able to turn the company around. It required us to fire a few people, spend more money on effective marketing channels, and completely redesign the product.

It wasn't easy and I wouldn't want to do it again, but I am always grateful that I learned the lesson of having a bias for action.

It is an easier life to dream and plan all day. You never have the risk of reality smacking you in the face to tell you that you are wrong. Without action, there is no pain.

But you also don't get any progress either.

Over the years, I have studied hundreds of successful people across different industries. They all share one common trait—the courage to act quickly and decisively.

No matter what industry you decide to pursue, I can promise you that every company wants someone on their team that gets things done. You don't have to be the smartest person or the most experienced, but if you can be the person that everyone relies on to get things done, then you will have a long, lucrative career.

In a world full of inaction, a bias for action stands out.

Dad

Effort creates action. Action creates results.

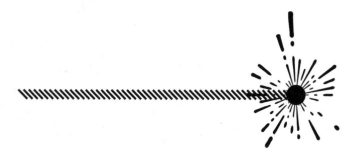

Finish what you start

Sofia & Leo,

Always finish what you start.

Even if it takes longer than you anticipated or it is more difficult than you initially realized. Completing a task or goal will give you confidence to take on the next one.

After Leo was born, your mother wanted to set a goal that would help her return to regularly exercising. She chose to run a half-marathon that was a few months away. This meant doing a few short runs during the week and then one longer run every weekend.

I watched her religiously stick to her running schedule for months. Each week brought a little progress. She was getting faster and running farther. Small wins stacking up to what she thought would be an epic race day.

There was only one problem.

Your mom and I both got a bad case of food poisoning the evening before her half-marathon. I thought it was the sushi we ate the previous night. She thought it was the pizza we ate for lunch that day. Regardless of the cause, we were each put out of commission.

We kept throwing up and having to use the restroom. Neither of us could keep any water down, let alone food. All we wanted to do was sleep for hours.

So that is what we did.

In between visits to the bathroom, we slept as much as possible. At some point around 4 a.m. on the morning of the race, it became obvious that she wouldn't be able to run the half-marathon a few hours later.

Your mom was devastated.

She had spent months training for her goal—run a half-marathon in under two hours.

But that wasn't going to happen on race day. Instead, we were confined to our apartment in an attempt to recover from the situation. I hated seeing your mom like that. Not only was she feeling sick, but she was disappointed that all her work had been wasted.

But that is not where the story ends.

A few days later, your mom decided that she was still going to run the half-marathon. She would run it the following Saturday in Central Park. There would be no official start or finish line. There would be no crowd to cheer her on. No water stations or snacks along the route.

Just your mom running by herself with a smartwatch to track her progress.

And that is exactly what she did. The next weekend she ran 13.1 miles in Central Park in under two hours. I took both of you to meet her at the new, imaginary "finish line."

Even though your mom didn't get to run the official race, she still made sure to finish what she started. It was important to her that she accomplished what she set out to do. It was important to both of us that our kids saw the importance of persistence.

I think fondly of that day. I was proud of your mom, but I was even more proud that we could show you all how to handle adversity.

Finish everything you start. If nothing else, it will make you proud that you kept that promise to yourself—and that's ultimately the thing that matters most.

Dad

It takes a level of obsession to achieve greatness.

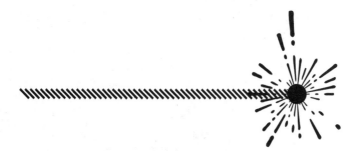

Luck is not real

Sofia & Leo,

Luck runs the world. At least it seems that way.

Successful people claim they got lucky. People who go through horrific events claim to have been unlucky. The notion of luck is everywhere.

But I hate to break it to you—luck is not real.

When I was deployed to fight the war in Iraq, there were multiple men injured. The injuries ranged from concussions to lost limbs. Some of these soldiers thought they were unlucky to have been the ones injured. Others thought they were lucky to have survived such a traumatic event.

Little did they know their outlook on their injuries would determine much about the future trajectory of their lives. The ones who self-prescribed that they were "unlucky" were more at risk for depression and a life of despair looking in the rearview mirror of what could have been.

The "lucky" ones, on the other hand, were able to express gratitude for a second chance at life and looked forward to accomplishing as much as they possibly could.

The person who claims they are unlucky has a pessimistic view of the situation, while the person who claims they are lucky has an optimistic view. See, luck is something that we conjure in our minds to grapple with the consequences of whatever life may throw our way.

When people talk about luck, they are usually talking about probability. What is the probability that a soldier is injured? That is a math question. We can analyze a number of factors and derive an answer to what the probability would be. You can't do the same thing with luck.

Luck is a psychological concept.

It is determined by how we view a situation. Two people can go through the same situation, and experience the same outcome, but have wildly different conclusions about their level of luck.

It is all in their mind.

In fact, academic studies now show that you can become luckier by simply telling yourself that you are lucky. Use this to your advantage and find the positives in any situation you go through.

And don't forget, luck is not real.

Dad

Luck is a psychology concept, not a mathematical one. Studies show that you become more lucky simply by thinking you're a lucky person. It is all mindset.

Chinese farmer

Sofia & Leo,

You have probably heard your mother and I utter the phrase "Chinese farmer" to each other many times throughout your life. These two words remind us of a simple parable we heard many years ago. Here is how Alan Watts retold the parable:

Once upon a time there was a Chinese farmer whose horse ran away. That evening, all of his neighbors came around to commiserate. They said, 'We are so sorry to hear your horse has run away. This is most unfortunate.' The farmer said, 'Maybe.' The next day the horse came back bringing seven wild horses with it, and in the evening everybody came back and said, 'Oh, isn't that lucky. What a great turn of events. You now have eight horses!' The farmer again said, 'Maybe.'

The following day his son tried to break one of the horses, and while riding it, he was thrown and broke his leg. The neighbors then said, 'Oh dear, that's too bad,' and the farmer responded, 'Maybe.' The next day the conscription officers came around to conscript people into the army, and they rejected his son because he had a broken leg. Again all the neighbors came around and said, 'Isn't that great!' Again, he said, 'Maybe.'

The moral of this story is that you never know if something is good or bad in your life at the time it is happening. Something may happen to you that appears to be negative in the moment, but later, you discover it was a blessing in disguise.

Take *Family Guy* creator Seth MacFarlane and actor Mark Wahlberg as examples. Both men were supposed to be aboard American Airlines Flight 11 on September 11, 2001. MacFarlane got drunk the night before, woke up late with a hangover, and missed the flight by 10 minutes. Wahlberg randomly decided to change his plans the day before and canceled his ticket.

Thankfully, neither man was on the airplane that was first to fly into the World Trade Center towers on 9/11. Chinese farmer. A seemingly negative situation—being late or canceling plans last-minute—had saved their lives.

Alternatively, there could be seemingly good news one day that you later learn has made your life more complicated or had some other kind of negative impact.

I cannot tell you how many friends have celebrated making lots of money very quickly, only to have their lives fall apart shortly after. They divorced their significant other. They lost custody of their children. People sued them. All the money eventually disappeared and what once seemed like a big victory ends in a nightmare.

Never get too excited, and never get too upset. Learn to approach every situation with a level head. The world has a weird way of working things out.

And, for better or worse, you'll never know whether something was a positive or negative development in your life until you have the benefit of hindsight.

Remember, the Chinese farmer knows best.

Dad

Claiming "good fortune" or "misfortune" is a psychological trick we play on ourselves to cope with random chance.

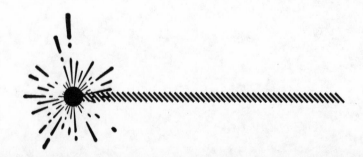

Two crappy pages per day

Sofia & Leo,

Everyone suffers with some degree of procrastination and inertia.

The cure for this predicament is two crappy pages per day.

When you are faced with a big project or a daunting task, don't try to accomplish everything at once. This is too difficult. Instead, break up the task into much smaller parts.

Bestselling author Tim Ferriss says that he tricks himself into writing his famously long books by simply writing "two crappy pages per day."

The pages don't have to be perfect.

By setting the goal as "crappy," anything you produce will meet the goal for the day. And when it comes to the amount of pages per day, it doesn't take much effort to create two of them.

So why is this such a powerful idea?

Because big things happen as a result of small progress.

This is a lesson that I apply almost every day.

I wrote this book of letters to you by writing a few letters each Sunday night. I created one of the most popular business podcasts in the world by recording three episodes each week. I built each one of our businesses by making just a little progress each day.

But the value of "two crappy pages per day" doesn't stop there.

I have also found that this framework lowers the pressure to perform. By lowering the pressure, the work ends up being higher-quality.

Low expectations bring high-quality work. Persistent progress leads to a large body of work.

Once you have the bulk of the work done, then you can begin diving into the details of perfecting the project. Isaac Newton had no idea he was talking about inertia at work when he said, "Things in motion, stay in motion."

Making worthwhile things is all about momentum.

You have to create it, then sustain it. Once you have the momentum, everything becomes easier. You get more ideas. You begin producing more. The finish line becomes more tangible and obvious.

Momentum creates energy, and energy creates results.

This all starts with two crappy pages per day. Slowly but surely, the ball of progress will begin rolling, and next thing you know, you will have a first draft.

Break the big projects into small ones. Identify the mini-milestones and then be disciplined enough to reach each one. Two crappy pages per day. That is all it takes.

Dad

A great way to formulate original ideas is to sit down and write every morning.

Force yourself to gather information, synthesize it, and produce an opinion on the topic.

The output is not nearly as important as the process of thinking and writing.

Don't compare yourself to the bottom of the bucket

Sofia & Leo,

Never compare yourself to the bottom of the bucket.

This was a lesson that I learned from my dad when I was in high school. He would say it to me over and over again. I didn't like hearing it at the time, but I realized he was right as I got older.

My goal in high school was to do the bare minimum necessary to keep my parents and my teachers off my back. I didn't care about the schoolwork. I realized early on that most of the material being taught in the classroom was not applicable to real life.

I was much more interested in the knowledge I would need once I left school. Street smarts over book smarts.

But my parents obviously had a different perspective.

They thought it was important for me to get good grades. It made them nervous that I may not get into college if I performed poorly in high school. So every time I received a report card, my parents and I went through the same sequence of events.

I would wait for as long as possible to show my parents the report card. My parents would eventually see it and be upset that I didn't get straight As. I would then tell them to relax because I still did better than a few kids in the class. My parents would be even more mad because they realized I was not optimizing to be the best, but rather, optimizing to not be the worst.

In other words, I wasn't playing to win. I was playing to not lose.

In my view, I wasn't trying to get the highest grades. I was just trying to do enough to get As and Bs. If there was an occasional C thrown in there, so be it. I wasn't getting Ds or Fs. I wasn't last in the class. As long as there was someone worse than me, then I was in decent shape.

Seems fair, right?

Wrong.

The problem is that this approach would make my parents incredibly mad. Even though I never got straight As, they were still disappointed every time I came home without straight As. They expected excellence from me. They wanted to see me do well at anything I spent time doing.

When I compared myself to the worst people in the class, my dad would remind me that I was not trying to improve and I was not trying to be the best in the class.

He would tell me over and over again, "Don't compare yourself to the bottom of the bucket."

If you compare yourself to those who are performing worse than you, you become complacent because you are better than them. If you compare yourself to those who are performing better than you, you become inspired to improve because you realize you have to catch up to them.

Your point of reference in a comparison is incredibly important. Make sure you are focused on the best and how you are going to catch up to them. That is the only way to become the best—you have to beat the best.

And you can't beat the best if you are focused on celebrating the fact that you are better than the worst.

Dad

If you want to build a large business and achieve significant success, you should treat the sport of business the same way a professional athlete would.

Hard work. Obsession with the craft. Studying the greats. Getting reps.

The formula works for both athletes and entrepreneurs.

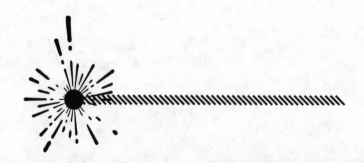

Tie your identity to your own name

Sofia and Leo,

Tie your identity to your own name.

This will ensure that no one can rob you of the most important thing you own—who you are.

Let me explain.

Most people tie their identity to external markers of success—their job title, their material possessions, even their relationship status. They become obsessed with thinking of themselves as a CEO, or a millionaire, or someone's spouse. As unfortunate as it may be, those identities are all tied to something that you could lose.

It may not seem like it, but it is incredibly dangerous to tie your name to activities, jobs, and roles.

It can be debilitating when the time comes to do something different. What does the CEO do when they retire? What happens to the millionaire when they lose their fortune during a recession?

What happens to your self-worth if your relationship falls apart and you are no longer known as someone's husband?

I am not sure why I always inherently knew this lesson, but thankfully I never got caught in the trap of tying my identity to anything but my name. I never thought of myself exclusively as a soldier. That was just something I did.

I never thought of myself as a player of a single sport. I played many sports and loved them all equally. Each job that I had, I knew it was only a stop along my journey to eventually creating my own businesses.

If you tie your identity to anything but your name, you lose your freedom. You become beholden to that thing. It becomes hard to leave. You don't want to disappoint people. You don't want to disappoint yourself.

I saw this firsthand when your mom was deciding whether to quit her job as a reporter and editor at *Fortune* magazine to pursue her newsletter venture full time. The hardest part for her was letting go of the notion that she would lose her identity as a magazine reporter. Suddenly, she would have to solely rely on her own name and reputation. That's when I reminded her, "You are most powerful when you tie your identity to your own name."

Your name is the most precious thing you have, and your reputation is the most sacred thing to protect.

As your mom recently said, "Create something that lets you tie your identity to something that actually matters—your own name. Nothing is more liberating, or more powerful."

Dad

The winning strategy moving forward will be to build everything under your own name and reputation.

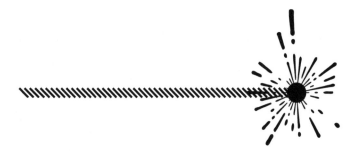

Two years of experience five times

Sofia & Leo,

You should focus on learning in your first few jobs.

Most people make the mistake of trying to make as much money as possible as soon as possible. Money is important, but it is not the most important thing. You want to set a strong foundation for the rest of your career.

This includes learning a skill, gaining experience, and building a network of talented people who have similar interests to you. It can be tempting to pick a job only for the money, but I have seen that story end horribly too many times to count.

Personally, I learned this lesson during my mid-20s. I had been fortunate to get a job as a product manager at Facebook. It was an incredible time to work there. The company had just gone public, and it was hitting new financial records every month. Anything we did as a company seemed to work.

I had chosen to go to Facebook instead of pursuing business school. The idea was that Facebook would give me a paycheck to learn real-life skills from the world's most talented team, while a business school would require me to pay to learn from academic professors steeped in theory.

But after about two years at Facebook, I started to get restless. I had built a reputation for myself and new job offers were coming in almost weekly. Some of them paid better than what I was earning at Facebook. Others paid less, but promised more responsibility and a larger team to manage.

I didn't know what to do. I loved Facebook. It felt like the place where I matured in my professional life. Facebook also had one of the highest densities of smart, ambitious people that I had ever seen.

As I agonized over the decision, I did what every kid eventually does—I called my dad.

The conversation was not very long. I explained the situation to him and asked him for advice. He said a few things that I don't remember, but one thing is still seared into my brain: "Make sure you don't work somewhere for 10 years, but only get two years of experience five times."

I knew I had to leave Facebook when he said that.

It was not what I wanted to hear, but it was exactly what I needed to hear. My dad was right. I had already learned about 80% of the things that I was likely to learn at the company. I had even had the pleasure of briefly working with most of the executives, including founder Mark Zuckerberg and then-Chief Operating Officer Sheryl Sandberg.

I knew if I stayed at the company longer than two years, I would be unlikely to leave in the next decade. That was the safe thing to do, but it wasn't the thing that would help me optimize for learning.

So within a few months of that phone call with my dad, I quit my job at Facebook and took a role at another technology company. This one gave me more responsibility and more money. Most importantly, it allowed me to accelerate my learning in a way that wasn't possible at Facebook.

When you are working for someone else, especially early in your career, you must optimize for learning. And you must know when it is time to leave. The worst thing you can do is get two years of experience five times.

Dad

I have optimized
my life around the
act of learning.

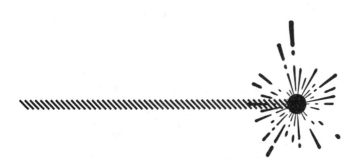

Life is full of power laws

Sofia & Leo,

An extraordinary life is made up of amazing moments.

Most people believe this means they need something amazing to happen every day. This is not true. In fact, you should expect the exact opposite.

Life is full of power laws.

Whether we are talking about accomplishments, experiences, relationships, or investments, the majority of the amazing things in your life will come from a relatively small amount of things you do.

The Pareto principle states that for many outcomes, roughly 80% of consequences come from 20% of the effort. I would take it even a step further—I believe 95% of the outcomes come from 5% of the inputs.

Let me explain.

You are unlikely to have hundreds, or thousands, of amazing relationships in your life. You will have an extraordinary life if you are able to maintain five incredible relationships with good people throughout your life.

The best example of this from my life is the relationship I have with your mom. This one person brings me more happiness than almost everyone else in my life combined. We are best friends. We enjoy traveling together and supporting each other's careers. And your mom is the best partner I could ask for when raising you, our children.

This principle doesn't only apply to relationships. You are unlikely to be able to have amazing experiences every single day. But if you take an insane trip somewhere in the world for two weeks every year, you will have had an extraordinary year by investing less than 5% of the days in the year in that trip.

Your mom and I once took a trip to Iceland to attend a friend's wedding. We visited volcanoes, swam in the Blue Lagoon, and flew high above the beautiful land in a helicopter. This trip was not only extraordinary, but it was something that we talk about fondly to this day.

Same goes for investing. I have found that approximately 95% of my financial returns have come from 5% of the decisions that I have made over the years.

What was the best financial decision I ever made? Buying bitcoin early. Although this was only one decision, it has led to substantial financial gains that put me in a position to create the life that I always wanted.

Once you understand that life is full of power laws, you will begin to make decisions differently.

It allows you to ignore the small decisions, while simply focusing on getting the big ones right. It only takes a few investments to build a significant portfolio. You only need five good personal relationships, or one amazing trip each year.

This makes your pursuit of an extraordinary life much more attainable.

Power laws may not fill the days, but they fill the years. And if you string together amazing years, you will end up with an extraordinary life.

Pursue the power laws.

Dad

Life is all about power laws. Relationships, experiences, financial returns. Find the 5% that delivers 95% and ignore the rest.

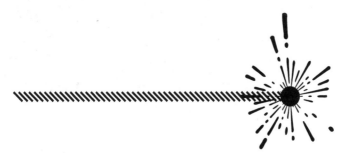

Take work off your boss's desk

Sofia & Leo,

The best people I have ever worked with all had one thing in common—they took work off their boss's desk.

It didn't matter what their job title was. The industry or the company didn't matter either. The best people always went above and beyond to help their bosses become more effective and efficient.

Think about it from the perspective of your employer.

They are hiring people to help them get a job done. There are customers to serve and work to do. Companies don't actually care who is doing the work as long as it is getting completed.

You know who does care though? Your boss.

They have a million things going on. If you can make their life easier, they will give you more responsibility. They will trust you, and, most importantly, they will like you.

When you get more responsibility, you not only get paid more money over time, but you also will learn faster. This is a great way to accelerate your career.

I haven't had too many jobs where I was working for someone else, but I distinctly remember when one of my employees took this approach. They would ask me every day what other tasks they could complete. At first, I would tell them, "Nothing," because I didn't know them well and had no clue if I could trust them.

But after a few days of this, I started to give them small projects they could complete in an hour or so after they finished their work for the day. The quality of the work was good. But the best part was that this individual would receive the task, go figure out how to get it done, and only come back to tell me that I didn't need to worry about it anymore.

Guess what happened? I started to give this person more and more responsibility.

Within months, this employee had gone from a recent college graduate to the general manager running one of our businesses. Why did I promote them so fast? They continued to prove to me that they could take on more responsibility and get the necessary tasks done quickly and effectively.

Ever since that experience, I tell all of our employees the same thing—figure out how to take work off your boss's desk.

That is the key to getting promoted, getting a raise, and achieving greater career success. The people who manage you are busy. There is more work to do than time in the day. If you can prove to be helpful, then they won't have a choice but to make you a more important part of the company.

Now, before you run out and start trying to be the hero at work, remember one important detail here: never outshine the master. I learned that from Robert Greene's *The 48 Laws of Power*.

You want to help your boss, but you still need to make them look good. Do the extra work for the respect of your boss, not the glory of your other colleagues. This is not an ego contest.

Take the work off their desk, but make sure everyone praises them. And you will have more success than you could ever imagine.

Dad

An easy way to advance your career is to get to the office early, do more work than your stated job responsibility, make your boss look good, and stay later than everyone else.

Be first in and last to leave.

Old school strategy that never fails.

Bad news doesn't get better with time

Sofia & Leo,

Bad news doesn't get better with time.

One of the biggest mistakes I see people make in life is waiting to communicate when something is wrong. They are scared to share the news or they are scared of the reaction from the person receiving the information.

Regardless of the reason, waiting to share bad news is almost always a terrible decision.

I had to learn this lesson the hard way early in my career. When I worked at Facebook, we had a situation where part of the product broke. I had no idea what had happened. Neither did anyone else on the team.

One minute, everything was working fine, but the next minute it seemed like users couldn't access our product. The definition of a nightmare situation.

Given that I didn't have a lot of experience handling a situation like this, I decided to do what seemed like the right thing—I tried to fix the problem. My first action was to work with our engineers to debug the issue.

Did Google block the website? Did something in the software code fail to render? Were users being redirected somewhere else? Maybe our analytics system was measuring incorrectly?

No matter how many questions we asked, we couldn't figure it out.

Eventually, I had no choice but to ask my boss for help. I went to him and explained the situation. To say he was livid would be an understatement. But he wasn't mad about the product being broken. He was mad that I knew about the problem for hours and didn't tell him.

As soon as I shared the problem with him, he called another team that was shipping a software update that day. It turns out the other team had written software that didn't work well with our product. Thankfully, once the other team was alerted to our issue, they were able to fix the problem within minutes.

Crisis averted.

But then the real learning started. My boss took me aside and explained that bad news doesn't get better with time. His point was that even if I had been able to figure out the problem by myself, those precious hours of downtime were costing the company money.

People within the organization needed to know what was going on.

To further make his point, my boss pointed to the fact that the problem was solved much quicker once I brought the rest of my team, including him, up to speed on what was happening.

He said, "People can't help you if they don't know there is a problem."

I never forgot that lesson. It is applicable to life, work, and relationships. When something goes wrong, immediately communicate the problem to all the key players. The more people you make aware of the problem, the more help you will receive in solving it.

Bad news doesn't get better with time. Your job in these situations is to put the word out that there is a problem. You will be surprised how quickly others will jump in to help.

Dad

Learn to communicate like your career depends on it.

It is the one skill that remains valuable regardless of the industry or job you pursue.

Maker's schedule, manager's schedule

Sofia and Leo,

It's not enough to be intentional about *what* you work on. You need to also be mindful of *how* you work on it.

Too many people mess this up. They allow everyone around them to be in charge of their calendar. Outsiders dictate what they work on, what meetings they attend, and where they have to be at any hour of the day.

This is a recipe for disaster.

The best way I have learned to manage my time comes from Paul Graham, who is widely considered to be one of the greatest early-stage technology investors in the world.

He shared the idea of a manager's schedule and a maker's schedule. Graham wrote on his blog:

> The manager's schedule is for bosses. It's embodied in the traditional appointment book, with each day cut into one-hour intervals. You can block off several hours for a single task if you need to, but by default you change what you're doing every hour.
>
> Most powerful people are on the manager's schedule. It's the schedule of command.
>
> But there's another way of using time that's common among people who make things, like programmers and writers. They generally prefer to use time in units of half a day at least. You can't write or program well in units of an hour. That's barely enough time to get started.
>
> When you're operating on the maker's schedule, meetings are a disaster. A single meeting can blow a whole afternoon, by breaking it into two pieces each too small to do anything hard in.

The key to implementing this idea is to truly understand what you are trying to accomplish. Can you get the work done efficiently in smaller segments of your day, or do you need long blocks of time?

Your calendar should match the work you are doing.

For years, I have implemented this strategy with great success. Every morning I block my schedule for writing. I don't take meetings during this time. I don't answer my phone. And I don't accept invitations for breakfast.

The morning is for writing.

If I am rushed, the work will suffer. If I have to write at a different time, the work won't be my best. I must protect my time or I won't accomplish my goals.

But then something interesting happens.

I abandon the maker's schedule at 10 a.m. each morning. Then, I become a manager. My calendar is packed until 5 p.m. with back-to-back 30-minute meetings.

Sometimes these are internal meetings. Other times they are with external people. Some of the people I know, and many I am meeting for the first time. We could be discussing new ideas, new companies, or new investments.

Anything goes after 10 a.m.

I can only do this because I was intentional about how I used my time in the morning. I leverage a maker's schedule to produce my highest-quality work, then I use a manager's schedule to run my businesses, explore new opportunities, and ensure that everyone else is doing their highest-quality work.

You can see how the maker's type of work benefits from longer, uninterrupted periods of focus. And you can see how the work of a manager can be done in shorter blocks.

Always ensure your schedule matches your work. It is the best way I know to get things done.

Dad

Time management is just another name for priority management.

Clear thinking can't happen in a messy room

Sofia & Leo,

It is hard to think clearly in a cluttered room.

It is hard to be detail-oriented when your office is a mess. It is difficult to stay on top of your priorities when you can't even stay on top of your living area.

Make sure you keep your space clean and well organized.

It took me until I was 17 years old to learn this lesson. Growing up, I always had a messy room. My parents would do their best to get me to clean it up, but within a day or two, it would be messy again.

Frankly, I just didn't care. I didn't see why it was important if my dirty clothes were neatly placed in the hamper or not, nor did I see a need in making my bed each morning or vacuuming the floor.

My bedroom was my personal space, and I thought my life would be the same, regardless of whether the room was clean or dirty.

That all changed when I went to basic training for the US Army.

During the few months of training, I had no choice—the Army demanded that my room was not only clean, but that it was spotless. They made sure I made my bed perfectly each morning. I had to hang my clothes with the proper distance between each hanger. And the floor was so clean that you could eat off of it.

Eventually, it became clear to me what was happening—I was learning discipline.

But it wasn't just discipline. I was learning to take pride in the possessions that I owned and the spaces that I inhabited. As I took more pride in these things, my life became more organized and successful.

You feed off your environment.

This is why it is so important to curate a space that fits your goals. If you want to do better work, make sure your work space is clean and organized. A study by the Princeton University Neuroscience Institute found that the brain's processing capacity is limited when a person is surrounded by clutter.

By keeping your environment free of clutter, Stanford researchers concluded from the same study that "you will be less irritable, more productive, distracted less often, and able to process information better with an uncluttered and organized home and office."

This idea is not exclusive to work though. You can use it for all aspects of your life.

If you want to work out more often, put a pair of dumbbells next to your bed so you pick them up before you go to sleep and when you wake up each morning.

Want to eat healthy? Make sure your kitchen has sunlight, real plants, and fresh fruits and vegetables in plain sight. You can design your life by designing your environment.

These may sound like things too small to make a difference, but they work. You can't help but fall victim to your surroundings.

Dad

Strive to be excellent in everything you do.

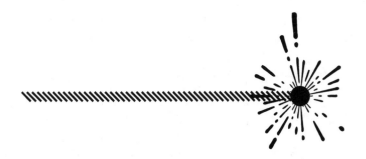

Management makes the rules, management changes the rules

Sofia and Leo,

Management makes the rules, which means management can change the rules.

This lesson was taught to me by my good friend and business partner Jason Williams. The first time he said it to me, I felt like I had just learned one of the secrets of the universe.

In business, you will constantly run into people who tell you something is not possible because of a random rule. Others will tell you, "This is how we have always done it." And some people will do things without even knowing why they are doing them.

These are all traps.

The people in charge usually have the ability to change the rules much more easily than you realize. If you are not in charge, seek out the people who are and explain to them why they should change things that don't make sense. If you are fortunate enough to be in charge one day, make decisions quickly to create the change necessary to accomplish the objective.

Early in my career, we had a rule at one of our companies that no one was allowed to take flights during business hours. The idea was that people should be working during business hours and then they could fly in the early or late hours of a day, so it didn't take away from the company's productivity.

For better or worse, I was adamant about enforcing this rule.

But one day, a young employee got a phone call that one of their parents was gravely ill in the hospital. The employee was distraught and wanted to go home to see their parents immediately, yet this would violate our travel rule.

Thankfully, this employee's manager saw that the employee was upset, learned what was going on, and raised the issue to me. I quickly told the employee that they should fly home as soon as possible and the company would pay for the flight.

The look on this employee's face was something I will never forget. They were shocked that I would authorize them to violate the well-known rule.

As I explained to the employee that day, certain rules are good ideas until they are not. The "no flying during business hours" made sense 95% of the time, but this was one of the 5% of times that it sounded ridiculous given the circumstances.

Since that experience, I have taken this lesson with me and applied it to business and my personal life. When something doesn't make sense, I try to figure out who is in charge of the situation and present them with an alternative option.

It is not always possible, but many times, I have seen management make changes on the fly to a variety of rules. This is exactly how leaders should operate. They are committed to a specific plan until they are presented with new information.

You should strive to be this type of leader as well. Management makes the rules, management can change the rules.

Dad

Most of the
"rules" in life are
things that were
either: (a) made
up; or (b) can be
changed if you
simply ask.

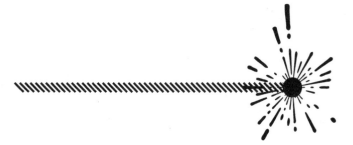

It's just business

Sofia & Leo,

People will take advantage of you in business if you let them.

This used to happen to me all the time. The problem was that I was too nice to others. Frankly, I didn't know any other way. I have always tried to be nice to everyone I meet.

That is how my parents raised me. Hopefully that is how your mom and I raised you.

The challenge in business is that some people you come in contact with will see your kindness as a weakness. They will try to take advantage of the situation. They can't help themselves.

If there is something to gain, someone will try it.

Be kind, but don't let people take advantage of you.

Here's what I do before a tough conversation: Minutes before I deliver a message outside of my normal approach, I whisper to myself, "It's just business."

Those three words changed everything for me.

The words didn't mean that I had to become a ruthless asshole. I wasn't immediately someone different than who I had always been. But those three words gave me license to prevent people from walking all over me or taking advantage of my kindness.

Once I started reminding myself that it was just business, people began to treat me differently.

They respected me more.

Everyone knows that I tend to be an easy-going, nice person. This makes it harder to manage people and hold them accountable when an individual is not performing up to the standard. In these moments, I whisper "It's just business" to myself, and then I have the tough conversation.

We once had a young employee who was consistently late to the office while underperforming in his work. I sat him down to explain how everything is related—if you fail to meet the standard in one area of work, you will fail to achieve success in other areas. It only took one conversation where I was very direct and honest to get this individual back on track.

If I allow bad performance to fester, I am disrespecting everyone else in the organization.

The big lesson? People respect those who respect themselves.

It is human nature. If you see an individual who is in-shape, well-groomed, and wearing nice clothes, you immediately form an opinion about this person. You think more highly of them because they obviously care enough to take care of themselves and ensure they look presentable.

This same idea applies to people intellectually as well.

When we see someone who knows their worth and can balance being kind but firm, we immediately think higher of that individual. Their self-confidence is attractive.

It is important to learn this skill.

You may find that whispering, "It's just business" works for you. Or maybe you need to find a different phrase. Whatever phrasing you use, make sure to remind yourself not to let anyone take advantage of you—in business or in life.

Be firm. Be kind. And let the bad actors go find someone else to pick on.

Dad

Most business problems are ultimately people problems.

Never ask someone to do something you are not willing to do

Sofia & Leo,

Never ask someone to do something that you are not willing to do yourself.

This advice may not be popular, but it is true. Leadership boils down to whether you can create a connection with the people you are leading. They need to trust and respect you.

But that is hard to do if you are always bossing them around.

Leaders who do this are doing what they think leaders are supposed to do, but in reality, they are hurting themselves. No one wants to follow a jerk.

A good example of this happened with a podcast that I ran in 2020. There were three parts to the workflow: 1) I would record an interview with a guest, 2) an audio and video editor would edit the footage into a final version, and 3) we would publish the episode across our media platforms.

The editing team was excellent. They always worked hard and produced amazing work.

But one day, the leader of the team came to me and said that everyone was getting tired from the pace of interviews we were doing. He claimed the editors didn't have enough time to edit everything before we were scheduled to publish the episodes.

Rather than get upset, I chose to do something the editing team didn't expect—I told them to take a week-long vacation.

Not only did I tell them to take the vacation, but I forbid them from editing any episodes for the week. Instead, I sat down after work every night and edited the episodes myself.

It was painfully difficult at first. I hadn't done the job in years. It took a while for me to find all the right information and remember how to use the editing software. After a few attempts, I was able to edit an episode and get it scheduled for publishing.

Remember, this was after I had recorded the interview earlier in the day and fulfilled all of the obligations I had with my job. I repeated the same thing the next day. And the next day. And the day after that.

Every single day for a week I was doing two jobs.

Why?

Because I knew that the editing team would have a hard time complaining if they saw their boss do their job on top of his own job. So that is exactly what I did.

Sure enough, when the editing team came back, they were shocked at how I had done both jobs. They couldn't believe it was possible.

I reminded them though—"I will never ask you to do something that I am not willing to do myself."

From that day forward, those editors were the hardest-working, most loyal employees I ever had. They had seen the lengths I was willing to go to in order to make sure the team was successful. They knew that I understood the difficulties and complexities of their job.

And they realized that they could trust me. I was never going to ask them to do something that I thought was beneath me.

This was one of the best leadership lessons that I ever discovered. People want to feel like they are part of a team, especially a team where the leader is going to look out for them. An easy way to do this is to show the team that you are capable and willing to do their job.

Never ask someone to do something that you are not willing to do yourself.

Dad

Leadership 101: Never ask your organization to do something you are unwilling to do.

Magnets attract opportunities

Sofia & Leo,

Humans often make the mistake of chasing things they want.

It could be a new car, a new job, or a new love interest. We trick ourselves into believing that we can convince the hiring manager to hire us. We tell ourselves that the cute person we've been chatting with will love us as long as we say the perfect thing in the next text message.

But this is all a lie.

You should become a magnet. Instead of chasing things you want, make people and things come to you. This will sound ridiculous at first, so let me explain how I did it in my life.

I was in my mid-20s when I started to have business success. The problem was that my success had happened inside a large company. Very few people outside the company knew who I was or what I had accomplished.

When I started investing in other people's companies, I found it hard to get meetings with the best entrepreneurs or convince them to accept my investment. The game is very competitive at the highest level. I grew so frustrated with the situation that I decided to change my tactics.

Rather than spend hours a day cold emailing prospective companies or investors, I began creating content on the internet. It started on Twitter (now known as X), but quickly spread to email, podcast, and YouTube. I would share ideas I had, lessons I had learned, or notes that I took after a call or meeting.

Frankly, I just started being myself on the internet.

This is when something really interesting happened—the more content I produced, the larger the audience that followed me became. Within a few years, I had millions of people following me across the different platforms.

But my goal was never to have a lot of followers. I wanted to get meetings with the best entrepreneurs and invest in their companies.

So I continued to talk publicly about interesting companies, developing industry trends, and my personal opinion on various news stories. As I continued, the entrepreneurs began to take notice. Some of them agreed with my opinions. Some of them disagreed. But eventually more of them learned who I was and were open to having a conversation.

As if that was not good enough, these founders were now interested in having me invest in their companies because I could talk about their company to my large audience online. Not only could I invest in their businesses, but I could give them exposure and distribution.

In hindsight, I see that I flipped the situation. Instead of spending my time chasing the thing that I wanted, I had figured out a way to get those entrepreneurs to come to me. I had become a magnet.

You must do the same thing in your life. Figure out what you want, and then design a situation where those people or things will be attracted to you.

If you want a certain job, build something interesting in that field. If you want to find a romantic partner, become a person with many interests that would attract the right kind of person. If you want to scale a successful business, create such a good solution to a painful problem that customers seek you out.

It is a much better situation when people chase you instead of you chasing them.

If you become a magnet, you will be shocked at what is possible.

Dad

Three simple ways to stand out from your peers:

1. Do the things you say you are going to do.

2. Respond quickly and concisely to people.

3. Make those around you successful.

What can I do to help you?

Sofia & Leo,

"What can I do to help you right now?"

It's a simple question that's created powerful opportunities in my career.

Throughout my life, I have had the chance to meet people from different industries, different geographies, and different stages of life. It was always obvious to me that I should ask the people with less experience how I could help them.

The responses would range from mentoring a young person, making introductions to someone I knew, investing money in the person's company, or making myself available to answer questions in the future. None of this is rocket science.

If you use it, you will find this question will change your life.

I have always been impressed by a young person who took the time to ask me how they could help me. In these situations, the young person knew that I could do much more to help them than they could do to help me. It didn't matter. They extended the offer anyway.

I almost never took the young person up on the offer, but the fact that they offered it stood out to me.

In a similar vein, I always made a point to ask people who were more successful than me how I could help them too. I doubted that I could do much, but maybe there was someone I could introduce them to who could provide feedback on a project or invest money in a deal.

A great example of this is when I met Robert Kiyosaki for the first time. He is the author of *Rich Dad, Poor Dad*, which is the best-selling personal finance book in history. I had read the book when I was 20 years old and considered Robert to have had a massive impact on my development as a young man.

I got the opportunity to talk with him in 2020 when I interviewed him for the first time.

We spent about an hour discussing various topics from personal finance to gold and bitcoin to central bank policies. It was a fascinating conversation, and I found Robert to be entertaining and interesting.

As the conversation was closing, and the interview recording had been shut off, I asked him if there was anything I could do to help him.

He responded with, "I would love your opinion on how I could better use social media to reach young people."

To be honest, I had not expected him to have any requests. I thought he would just smile politely and say there was nothing. But here was a big opportunity. The guy who had written one of my favorite books was now asking for my help.

I immediately sprung into action. After sharing a few initial ideas on the call, I spent hours putting together a document filled with ideas over the next few days. I sent it to Robert and his team.

Within weeks, Robert asked me to get on phone calls with him, his team, his advisers, and some of their business strategists. They spent time explaining their business and goals, while I spent time sharing my ideas for how they could leverage social media.

It was an incredibly cool experience. I ended up building a friendship with one of the best authors in the world because I was respectful enough to ask, "How can I help you?"

Robert and I remain friends today. We text periodically. He shares his thoughts on various current events, and I send him feedback on how his team communicates on social media.

This would have never happened without that simple question.

Don't forget to ask people how you can help. It doesn't matter how successful they are. You'll be surprised by what can happen.

Dad

The more you help other people become successful, the more success finds you.

Call your friends for no reason

Sofia & Leo,

Many people in the world are lonely.

They lack a group of friends that they can talk to on a periodic basis. It leaves them wondering if anyone cares about them. And when something negative happens in their life, they find themselves unable to talk with anyone about it.

That is the irony of a hyper-connected world. This situation sucks for the people who are in it.

You can help your friends avoid this disaster though. Call one or two friends each week for no reason. Check in on them. Ask them how they are doing. Ask about work, their relationships, and their family.

I have been doing this for years, and I never regret picking up the phone.

There are two secrets that I will share with you about these random, unprompted conversations.

First, they go exponentially better if you are genuinely curious about how the person is doing. Your friends aren't stupid. They know when you are doing something out of obligation.

Don't try to fool your friends—call them only if you actually want to hear their life updates.

Second, these conversations will be one of the most selfish things you do. You will almost always leave the conversation more energized. You will wonder why you didn't call sooner.

It feels good to talk with old friends or colleagues. These individuals probably know you better than the people you spend time with today. Why? They know the old version of you, which is before you got smarter and more experienced.

This can be helpful because they will keep you grounded. It is easy to reminisce about the good times that you all shared. These calls will often be full of smiles and laughter.

Life is chaotic, and we all get busy. Take the time to reach out. It is important.

You will hold on to friendships longer. It will make you happy. And you will be motivated to continue progressing in your life so you have good news and positive updates to share at the next call.

Pick up the phone. Make the call.

Dad

A great conversation is priceless.

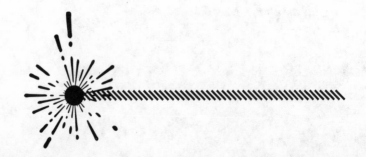

Make people talk about themselves

Sofia and Leo,

People love to talk about themselves.

An easy way to make friends is to simply ask them questions. Ask them where they are from. Ask them what they do for a living. Ask them about their family or their hobbies.

As the bestselling author Dale Carnegie wrote in his book *How to Win Friends & Influence People*, "Talk to someone about themselves and they'll listen for hours."

When I first read Carnegie's advice, I didn't believe it could work. It was too simple. How could someone talk about themselves for hours? Well, let me tell you from experience, most people do it without thinking.

I have been fortunate enough to meet politicians, musicians, celebrities, and athletes. I have interviewed many of the most successful people over the years. And I have had the pleasure of meeting thousands of everyday citizens in various countries.

They all share one common trait—they love to talk about their unique life experience.

The tricky part is getting someone to trust you enough to share their life story. A helpful tool I have discovered is to implement Toyota's "Five Whys" framework when meeting someone new.

Toyota, the Japanese automotive manufacturer, pioneered the idea of asking "Why?" five times in order to uncover the root cause of a problem. They were focused on their manufacturing facilities, but the technique can be applied to many different aspects of life. I have been using the same technique for years to uncover the most interesting aspects of a person.

Ask someone a question. When they answer, follow up with another question. It can be as simple as, "Why…?"

And then keep going. Ask "Why?" five times or more if you have to.

The more questions you ask, the more layers you will uncover about a person's life.

As the conversation comes to an end after five minutes or five hours, the person you are talking to will walk away feeling good. And you will have learned something new.

You can't learn something new if you spend all your time talking about yourself.

This may sound like an easy lesson to implement, but you must remember that you are human, and you'll be tempted to make the conversation about you. Fight the urge.

You already know your story, so spend the time to learn someone else's.

Dad

Great communication skills make business and life easier.

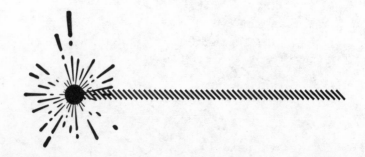

Genuinely caring is a life hack

Sofia & Leo,

You must genuinely care about the things you do in life.

This is a great way to ensure you live an extraordinary life. It is true of your work, your relationships, and your hobbies.

But you can't fake it. Not only can other people tell whether you are truly passionate about something or not, but the hardest person to lie to is yourself.

By caring about your work, you will inevitably work harder on it, spend more time learning new skills, and ultimately be more successful over the long run. By caring about your relationships, you will have more fun with your friends and a stronger bond with your loved ones. And by caring about your hobbies, you will get more enjoyment out of these activities.

Since you can't fake it, you have to discover what you are truly passionate about.

Take me as an example—throughout childhood I thought I was going to be a lawyer when I grew up. I knew I was good at formulating arguments and debating ferociously. I had strong analytical skills and paid attention to detail, which lends itself nicely to understanding complex legal rules.

Where did I get this idea about becoming a lawyer?

Everyone in my life told me I would make a great lawyer. My parents, teachers, sports coaches, and almost any other adult I interfaced with. They were all in agreement—I was destined to be a lawyer.

But a big problem started to develop over time.

As I got older, I realized that I would make a good lawyer, but I had almost no interest in attending law school, passing the bar exam, or spending my professional career debating people in a courtroom.

Simply, I didn't care about being a lawyer.

You can imagine how big of a shock this was to people around me when I decided I would not pursue the lawyer path. Instead, I started to think about what I truly cared about. Where did I spend my free time? What did I feel energized about when talking to friends? What information did I seek out daily to stay up-to-date?

Each one of these answers pointed me towards business and technology.

I was obsessed with everything related to starting companies. It didn't matter if we were talking about the founders who created a company, the investors who funded it, or the industry analysts who studied trends about where the technology was headed.

This is why I decided to pursue a career in early-stage technology companies—I cared.

Because of this, I truly feel like I have never worked a day in my life. Warren Buffett once said he "tap dances to work" every day. That makes two of us.

Caring about what you do gives you an advantage in life. Don't squander it.

Dad

Be curious, be genuine, and be honest.

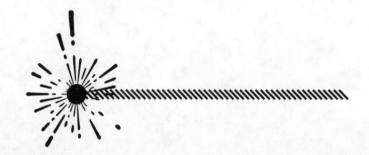

Get on the plane

Sofia & Leo,

As the world gets more digital, remember that sometimes you should get on a plane and visit people in person.

This is a key ingredient to living an extraordinary life.

There is nothing like face-to-face interaction with another human being. It not only creates stronger bonds between you and others, but it also increases the odds that you will accomplish whatever you have set out to do.

The first time I learned this was when I was fundraising for a venture capital fund. Historically, everything I did was over the phone or through video calls. My thought process had been, "Why should we waste time traveling if we have so much innovative technology that allows us to communicate from different locations?"

That strategy had served me well, but a salesman changed my mind.

This man was responsible for helping me to raise the capital. When I told him that I was planning to make phone calls and talk to people on my computer, he laughed at me. He couldn't help himself.

It seemed so absurd to him. So after a few conversations, he convinced me to take a trip with him to Virginia to go visit a few prospective clients in person. At 6 a.m. on the day of these meetings, I left New York City on a plane and flew to Washington DC.

Throughout the course of the day, we went office to office meeting various people and organizations. Without a doubt, these conversations were higher quality and more effective than virtual meetings.

Part of the benefit was that the people we were meeting with knew how serious we were if we had been willing to fly to town to see them. They also appreciated the fact that they could look me in the eyes, shake my hand, and get a sense for who I was as a person.

It may sound old-school, but it worked.

By the end of the day, we had secured the first commitments for the venture capital fund. In fact, those first commitments ended up being the largest investors in the entire fund. Not bad for a day trip that only took a few hours on a plane.

Business is not the only time this lesson can be applied.

A few years later, I wanted to interview John McAfee. He was a legendary tech entrepreneur who had become infamous for a life of drugs and crime. John and his wife were living a life on the run on a boat in the Caribbean.

When I got in touch with them, I offered to fly anywhere in the world to meet them. They were immediately much more serious about making the meeting happen. John's wife told me where they would be in the Bahamas and what date they would arrive.

I booked my flight minutes later and sent them confirmation.

That trip was one of the coolest and craziest things I have ever experienced. I spent hours meeting with John aboard the boat. We talked about his life, his perspective on current events, and what he hoped his legacy would be.

I was reminded how fragile life is that day. John McAfee, who had once been a billionaire, was now living life hiding from authorities in foreign countries. As sad as it was to see that side of John, I also saw a man who was married to his principles and was dedicated to squeezing every ounce of enjoyment out of his remaining days.

None of those lessons would have happened if I had not gotten on the plane and met him in person.

Make sure you do the same thing.

It is easy to stand out in a digital world by putting a premium on face-to-face interactions. Get on the plane. Make the effort. Create the extraordinary.

Dad

Invest in relationships and experiences.

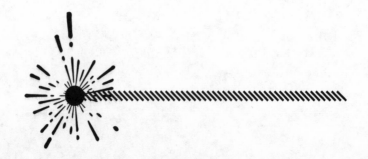

Spend time with your peers

Sofia and Leo,

Learn to value your peers more than your heroes.

This is counterintuitive, so let me explain. Every young business person becomes interested in successful people at some point. These successful people could be famous investors, billionaire CEOs, or individuals who have risen to the top of their chosen industry.

There is a fascination that develops with how these people became successful. You will want to meet them and learn. You will want to become their friend. You may even dream that one day you could go into business with one of them.

Anything is possible, but I have found that people over-index on their heroes and under-index on their peers.

When I was in college, I didn't care who was in class with me. I wanted to meet the people who were donating millions of dollars to the university. When I was early in my career, I didn't pay attention to the entry-level employees working beside me. I wanted to meet and spend time with the executives. When I started investing, I was less interested in the other young investors and much more excited about being introduced to the experienced, wealthy investors.

But as I started to meet more of my heroes, I noticed something interesting.

They all talked about their friends who they had known for 20 years. If they wanted to get something done, they were at a point in their career where they would call up a friend who was the CEO of a specific company or an investor behind a big deal. They had all grown up in the business together. These relationships were built on decades of trust.

Many of the people you go through life with—from school to work—will end up being one of your greatest resources as you become more successful. You not only want to have a large network of successful people that you can reach out to when appropriate, but you also want to have a group of ambitious friends who you can trust.

Meeting your heroes and learning from them is great. You should try to learn as much as you can from everyone you meet. Just don't confuse your hero for your friend. They will always look at you as the young kid who is trying to figure it out. Maybe they will do you a favor every once in a while, but you can't count on your heroes to be there for you over decades.

That is what your circle of trusted friends is for. You have to spend time with them. Get to know them. Meet their families. Understand what drives them. Take note of their goals. Be interested in who they are as a person. Find deals to do together.

The more you all do together, the more you will learn to trust each other. The good deals will be fun and the bad deals will be where you solidify your friendship.

Don't fall into the trap of thinking your heroes are more important than your peers. I have found the exact opposite to be true in my life.

Dad

Spend more time with your peers than your heroes— you can learn from both, but you will call peers more often than heroes over time.

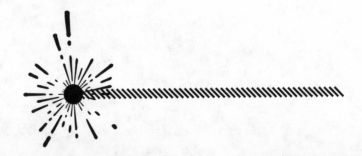

Host dinner for interesting people

Sofia and Leo,

An extraordinary life is filled with extraordinary people and extraordinary conversations.

One way to ensure you get to experience both of these often is to host dinners in your own home. When you do this, you control the guest list, the cuisine, and the direction of the conversation. You get to invite whoever you want, and if you want to be around interesting people, then that's who you invite to your dinner.

Worried that you can't get interesting people to a dinner? Let me tell you a secret.

You can find one interesting person that other people will want to meet or be around. Tell this person that you are going to host a dinner in their honor. Everyone loves to be honored, so they will likely agree to attend.

Next, you can tell other interesting people that you want to invite them to a dinner in honor of the main interesting person. By using your honoree's name, you will be able to convince many other interesting people to attend.

Interesting people love to be around interesting people.

But now that you have a few interesting people coming to your dinner, what do you do to make it fun, memorable, and… interesting? Make sure you come prepared with a few questions to pose to the group so they have something to talk about.

Your mother and I have been doing this for years. We bring together friends from different industries. Some people we have known for years, while others only a few days. If someone is interesting, they are likely to get an invite.

But the chemistry of the group and the success of the dinner largely hinge on the questions.

My favorite question to pose to the group is, "What's one thing you believe privately that you'd be scared to share publicly out of fear of provoking outrage?" This forces people to reveal their true thoughts about something they think is controversial.

Other good questions are, "What is one thing you have recently changed your mind about?" or "If you could hold on to just one memory for the rest of your life, what would it be?"

These questions force people to think more deeply than normal. It requires someone to be honest and vulnerable with those around them. And the funny thing is, once people have answered my favorite questions above, the conversation then naturally flows to other areas for the rest of the evening.

This all helps to pull together a group of interesting people that leave dinner knowing each other better.

Life should be fun. A great way to ensure you have fun is to host regular dinners and invite the people you want to get to know better.

You will be shocked at how many people are starving for interesting conversation with interesting people. One unintended consequence of hosting these regular dinners is that friendships, business deals, and new jobs have formed as a result of the serendipity that comes from going to dinner with strangers.

When in doubt, host a dinner and be a magnet for extraordinary conversations.

Dad

A great dinner question that almost always spurs deeper, more valuable conversations: What is the most impactful thing you have ever done for someone else and why did you do it?

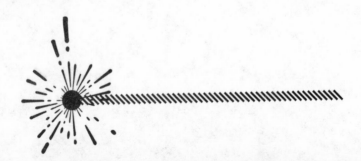

Surround yourself with compounders

Sofia & Leo,

Surround yourself with compounders.

Compounders are people who focus on compounding knowledge, health, wealth, and deep relationships over decades.

These friends are hard to find, but invaluable when you do.

They will force you to level up your game. Conversations with these individuals are higher quality. Their success will inspire you to accomplish more. And you will get the added benefit of learning from your successful friends' wins and losses along the way.

One of my compounder friends, let's call him Martin, runs a very large technology company that does hundreds of millions of dollars in revenue.

He wasn't always this successful though. This is his third startup. The successful version of the company today is the third or fourth iteration of the same idea.

How did he do it?

Martin has an insatiable desire to learn and improve. He is constantly reading books, listening to podcasts, talking to successful founders or investors, and asks more questions than almost anyone I know.

As Martin learns new things, he shares them with me. I do the same with him. Right after a phone call, one of us may text the other a lesson or two we took away from the conversation. If one of us reads a book or article that has an insight in it, we do our best to immediately share it with each other.

The lessons could be related to business, fitness, relationships, or happiness.

Gather information. Share it. Repeat.

If I did this with almost anyone else in the world, especially at the pace and intensity that Martin and I follow, the other person would ask me to stop. Most people aren't obsessed with learning, nor do they have the patience and dedication to compound improvement for decades.

This is why it is so important to find a small group of these compounders and then work together for a long period of time to see everyone improve.

Motivational speaker Jim Rohn once said, "You're the average of the five people you spend the most time with."

If you want to become a compounder of knowledge, health, wealth, and deep relationships over decades, then you have to hang out with the people who are already compounding.

The quality of your future depends on it.

Dad

I try to surround myself with compounders— people who focus on compounding knowledge, health, wealth, and deep relationships over decades.

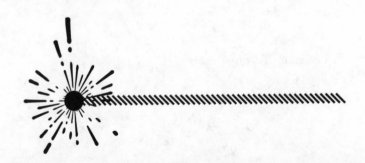

No one is thinking about you

Sofia & Leo,

Don't waste your time wondering what other people think about you.

The truth is that no one else is thinking about you. They are all too self-absorbed in their own worlds. They don't have time for you because they are too focused on themselves.

There was a period of time in my life when I didn't understand this.

Throughout high school, I always wondered what everyone else thought about me. What did my friends think about me? What about my teachers? What about college admissions officers? What about my coaches? How about the girls that I liked? Or the girls that I didn't like?

It was all a huge waste of time.

Not only were these people not thinking about me, but even if they had been, it wouldn't have mattered. I couldn't tell you the names of 90% of these people today. They all went their separate ways in life, and I hope they are doing well, but I haven't thought about a single one of them until I sat down to write this letter.

It is easy to drown ourselves in worry about how others perceive us. We think that a single decision or action can change that external perception.

But an interesting lesson you will learn along the way is that the people who know you well won't care about any one action or decision, and the people who do care about those individual decisions or actions aren't the type of people whose opinion you should care about.

Living your life trying to please others is the exact opposite of living an extraordinary life. That is a form of mental prison where there are no winners.

Don't waste time worrying what other people think. You will eventually realize they are too busy to think about you—and that is freeing.

Dad

Your life changes once you realize that no one else's opinion matters as long as you know who you are.

Fire boring
friends

Sofia & Leo,

You can't live an extraordinary life surrounded by boring people.

This is a hard truth, but it is still a truth. You have to find people who are ambitious. People who are pursuing epic challenges. People who squeeze every second out of life. And people who are living their own extraordinary lives.

But we all only have room for so many friends. Experts say your brain can't manage relationships with more than 150 people. That includes people you work with, people you have met over the years, and people you hang out with constantly.

To make room for the best people in your life, you must learn to fire your boring friends.

This doesn't mean these people are bad people. It doesn't mean they aren't great friends. But it does mean they are boring, which is unhelpful in your pursuit of living an extraordinary life.

If you were optimizing for being friends with as many people from high school as possible, you wouldn't fire your boring high school friends. If you were optimizing for having a large group of friends in a single industry, you wouldn't fire the boring friends from that industry.

But if you are optimizing for living an extraordinary life, you have to fire all the boring friends and find people living extraordinary lives. If your boring friends really care about you, they will understand.

Fortunately, I was able to find many of these people organically throughout the years. I have friends who are elite soldiers, world record-holders, founders of multi-billion dollar companies, authors of best-selling books, artists who sell out arenas, globe-trotters, and parents raising incredibly successful families. These friends have gone on to achieve more extraordinary moments than they could have ever imagined.

It is nearly impossible to hang out with these people and not be inspired to accomplish more in life.

Ultimately, this is what you are looking for. You want to be around people who are constantly pushing you to achieve more and get you closer to your goal of living an extraordinary life.

Humans tend to suffer from entropy. As we get older, it becomes easier to stay at home on a Friday night. We are less interested in taking the 100th trip to a foreign city. The messiness of life, including family, work, and hobbies, starts to get in the way of the things we previously wanted to accomplish.

You have to fight the entropy. You have to rage against the trend.

Surrounding yourself with a solid group of people living extraordinary lives will help you do this. Boring friends do the opposite. They will merely reinforce the status quo.

The status quo is the enemy. There are billions of people who will live the status quo life. That path is already worn down from how popular it has become.

Our goal is to blaze our own path—to find our way in the world by doing the things that we will tell our grandchildren about. The extraordinary life is not for everyone. Actually, it is not for most people.

It requires a degree of dedication that is too difficult for most people to exhibit. And it requires you to fire your boring friends. You don't have to be rude about it. In fact, you may not even have to say anything at all.

I have found that you can fire people from your life by simply putting space between you and them. You will grow apart over time. They will pursue the life they want to live, and you will be free to chase the extraordinary life you desire.

Remember, you can't be extraordinary if you're surrounded by mediocre people.

Dad

Surround yourself with winners.

Find a few people destined for greatness and sprint to keep up with them.

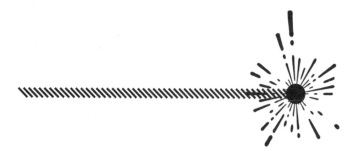

Respect other people's time

Sofia and Leo,

Time is the most valuable asset in the world.

I didn't understand this for the first half of my life. Fortunately, I read a story online that changed my perspective. The story started with someone asking "Are you richer than Warren Buffett?"

At the time, Buffett was one of the three wealthiest people in the world. He reportedly had more than $100 billion, so only two people in the entire world could answer with, "Yes, I am richer than Warren Buffett."

But, as you probably guessed, this was one of those trick questions.

The point of the story is that Buffett is over 90 years old. No amount of money could reverse his advancing years. And so the next question was whether you would switch lives with Warren Buffett—tomorrow you can wake up with more than $100 billion, but you have to also immediately age to over 90 years old.

Would you do it?

No sane person would make this trade. It would be nice to have $100 billion, but no one would trade decades of their life for it—especially since you wouldn't have much time to enjoy the money.

This makes you wealthier than Warren Buffett today. You have more time than him, and time is worth much more than money.

So why am I taking the time to explain how important time is?

Because people always think about the value of money and how they'd like more of it. But until we are posed the simple and obvious question about Warren Buffett above, we don't often think about how time is in fact much more valuable, and we ought to be thinking about how to maximize our time.

It follows that one of the most important things you can do in life is to respect other people's time.

Don't ask people to do things that will waste their time. Do your best to never be late. And if you're going to be late, or if you need to cancel, make sure you tell the other person as soon as you know.

When I was playing football in college, one of our coaches used to say, "Five minutes early is on time and on time is late." I never forgot that.

By respecting other people's time, they will realize that you are a serious person. You understand the value of time. And something funny will happen, the other person will do their best to avoid wasting your time too.

People tend to mimic what they see others do.

Time is valuable. Don't let a second go to waste.

Dad

Be direct, be honest.

Respect people's time, they'll respect yours.

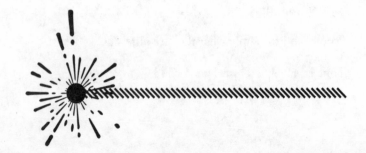

You don't get if you don't ask

Sofia & Leo,

Too many people are timid in life. They are scared to be ambitious. They avoid anything that could put them in a position to live an extraordinary life.

Don't fall for this trap.

You can get whatever you want out of life. You just have to ask.

I first heard the phrase "You don't get if you don't ask" when I was in my early 20s. It almost seemed too simple. Was that really the secret to life? You just ask for things and then they happen?

It couldn't be that easy.

Well, what I have found is that there is 0% chance of most things happening if you don't ask. You are essentially guaranteed to fail in the accomplishments, experiences, and milestones that you aren't willing to go after.

But the things you do ask for, regardless of who you are asking, have a higher probability than 0%.

The chances may still be low, but at least they aren't zero.

There have been many times I have used this knowledge to my advantage. I was once selling a Tesla Model Y and the dealership gave me a quote for what they were willing to pay me. It seemed like a low-ball number, but the dealer promised it was an attractive number.

Instead of accepting, I asked if he could go back to his manager and ask for a higher purchase price. About 20 minutes later, the man returned with an offer for a few thousand dollars more. If you don't ask, you don't get.

Another time, I was negotiating my salary at a big company early in my career. I didn't have a lot of money at the time and this job would have required me to move across the country. After we discussed how much I would be paid, I asked the recruiter if the company could give me money to cover the cost of the cross-country move.

The recruiter told me they didn't think it was possible, but I asked them nicely to just go ask their boss. Two days later, I was signing a contract to take the new job, which happened to include a $10,000 stipend to pay for the move.

You don't get if you don't ask.

This lesson doesn't only pertain to money. You can use it in many different areas of your life. For example, when I met your mother for the first time at a coffee shop on a Thursday morning, I really enjoyed the conversation.

She had mentioned that she would be going out of town that weekend and I didn't want to wait to see her until the following week. So what did I do? I asked her if she was free to go to dinner the same day.

Some people would have been scared to ask such a forward question, but I knew, "You don't get if you don't ask."

When you want something in life, ask for it. You'll be surprised how many times you get it.

Dad

You will be surprised at what you can receive if you just ask.

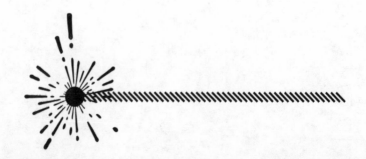

Compete, don't complain

Sofia & Leo,

Things will go wrong in your life—sometimes very wrong.

It happens to everyone. You won't be able to avoid it.

Don't worry though. Few things are insurmountable although they may seem that way in the heat of the moment.

You can manage a bad situation by being intentional about how you respond to it.

A phrase that I am fond of repeating to friends is, "Compete, don't complain." When things go wrong, it can be easy to feel sorry for ourselves. We think the world isn't fair. We don't understand why the bad thing has happened to us.

The same is true when things get hard.

Adversity is painful. But make sure you don't become a complainer. Complainers are very good at talking, but they are very bad at acting. They spend the majority of their time finding someone else to blame for the situation. They are allergic to personal responsibility.

Complainers are pessimistic by nature. They see the glass as half empty. It is hard to become a winner in life if you always think you are a victim. It is even harder to win if you focus all of your energy on complaining.

The people I admire most are the competitors. Regardless of the odds they face, these individuals are ready to do whatever it takes to win. They have a positive attitude. They are constantly thinking about their next move. There is no time to sulk or complain.

Competitors are too busy acting.

I heard former Navy SEAL officer Jocko Willink say that he responds to any problem with the word, "Good."[1] He explained why:

> When things are going bad, there's going to be some good that will come from it…
>
> Oh, the mission got canceled? Good… We can focus on another one.
> Didn't get the new high-speed gear we wanted? Good… We can keep it simple.
> Didn't get promoted? Good… More time to get better.
> Didn't get funded? Good… We own more of the company.
> Didn't get the job you wanted? Good… Go out, gain more experience, and build a better resume.
> Got injured? Good… Needed a break from training.
> Got tapped out? Good… It's better to tap out in training than tap out on the street.

---

1 nickglassett.com/jocko-willink-good-transcript

Got beat? Good… We learned.

Unexpected problems? Good… We have to figure out a solution.

That's it. When things are going bad: Don't get all bummed out, don't get started, don't get frustrated. No. Just look at the issue and say: "Good."

This is a great way to look at life. No matter what happens, you can complain or you can compete. The competitors tend to be the winners—in business, relationships, and life. They are too busy focused on finding and executing a solution. There is no time to complain.

You will face many obstacles and challenges in your life. Use them as opportunities. It is all about perspective. A problem can't hurt you unless you are complicit in the damage.

Compete, don't complain.

Dad

Stop complaining.
Start competing.

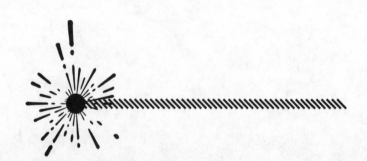

Puzzles, not problems

Sofia & Leo,

Problems are often talked about as something negative—something to be avoided at all costs.

But problems can actually be fun. In fact, I get excited when I encounter a problem. That's because I prefer to think of problems as puzzles waiting to be solved.

When you both were babies, you would cry from time to time. That is what babies do. Rather than get frustrated or upset, I would always remind your mom that there were generally three reasons why a baby would be crying—they were hungry, they were tired, or they needed their diaper changed.

A baby's cry suddenly went from a problem to a puzzle that could be solved by systematically checking those three potential causes. This approach made it easier on your mother and I when you were newborns.

This is not the only time I have used this framework.

Problems arise in business on a daily basis. People can easily grow frustrated and lose their emotional control. They feel like something outside of their control has screwed up their plans.

It could be a mistake by a colleague. It could be a decision by a competitor. Maybe a business partner or vendor has a different idea on how to execute something.

Regardless of the details, if you view a situation as a problem it will become difficult to navigate. You are starting from a negative viewpoint on the set of facts. The better way to approach these situations is the same way you'd approach a puzzle—with a creative mind.

Years ago, I was trying to secure an office for one of our businesses in New York City. The landlord was choosing whether to rent it to us or to another group. On paper, the other tenant was the better choice. Their business had been around longer, they had much more cash on their balance sheet, and their group was well-known across the city with a solid reputation.

But you know me—the odds being stacked against us wasn't going to stop me. It made me want to compete even more.

I approached the situation like a puzzle. What actions could I take to turn this potential problem into a puzzle that I could solve and win?

I knew who the decision-maker was at the landlord's business, so I scoured my network looking for mutual connections. Thankfully, there were many. I reached out to every single one of them and asked them to send a note to the decision-maker vouching for us. Remember my advice elsewhere in this book: If you don't ask, you don't get.

It wasn't one or two notes. The decision-maker must have received 15 or 20 of them. It was impossible to ignore how many people were reaching out. The social pressure alone caused the landlord to realize we may be the right tenant for the space.

We only made progress because of the way we approached the situation.

I don't have problems. I have puzzles to solve. And the only way to solve a puzzle is to go one piece at a time. If you remember this throughout your life and career, you'll be prepared for any "problem" you encounter.

Dad

You either think the world can be better in the future and you work to make that happen... or you think the world is guaranteed to decline and you sit around complaining.

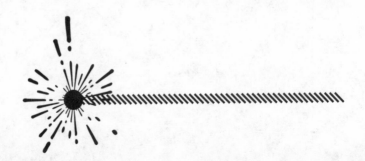

Most people would dream of having your problems

Sofia and Leo,

Most people would dream of having your problems.

Every human on earth deals with adversity. We all have dreams and goals, but not all of them pan out. Some people are born into poverty. Others have horrific medical conditions they must face. Many people find themselves in less than ideal situations because of decisions they made in their life.

Regardless of whether you are struggling or doing well, everyone has problems.

The philosopher Socrates said it best: "If all our misfortunes were laid in one common heap, whence everyone must take an equal portion, most people would be content to take their own and depart."

Newspaper columnist Regina Brett paraphrased this idea even better with, "If we all threw our problems in a pile and saw everyone else's, we'd grab ours back."

I have found this idea to be true multiple times in my life.

Once, I had to get surgery on my left hand, so I went to visit a doctor at the Veterans Affairs Hospital in Durham, North Carolina.

As I walked through the hospital, while telling myself how much I was not looking forward to wearing a cast for the next eight to ten weeks, I began noticing the other patients in the hospital. Many of them had lost an arm or a leg in combat.

All of a sudden, my slightly injured hand seemed like a miniscule problem compared to the alternative.

This made me think about how fortunate I was. I lived in the United States of America, the most prosperous country in the world. I didn't worry about where my next meal would come from, nor did I worry about clean drinking water or heat in the winter. I had a loving family and an amazing set of friends. And I had unlimited economic and social mobility in front of me.

Whatever small problems I may face seemed immaterial to the problems faced by billions of people globally.

After having this insight, I have tried to remind myself throughout my life that I can always throw my problems in the pile. It won't solve them though. And exchanging my problems for someone else's will likely put me in an even worse position.

It may sound counterintuitive, but with the right perspective, you will start to see your problems as a blessing.

And that is exactly how it should be.

Dad

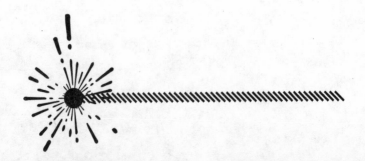

Adversity creates opportunity for an optimist.

Every play is drawn up to be a touchdown

Sofia & Leo,

Life has a way of not following the plans you set out for it.

I learned this lesson while playing college football. When the coaches drew up a play in practice, every play was designed to score a touchdown.

They had made sure each play accounted for every defender. Whatever we faced, our coaches had the answer.

Literally every play was a touchdown. They never drew a play that didn't work.

But then, it was game-day.

We would line up against our opponents and run play-after-play. Most of them didn't end up in touchdowns though. Something would go wrong. It could be an unexpected response from the other team. It could be that one of our teammates didn't do their specific job on the play. Or the coaches could have called the wrong play considering what the defense was doing.

Regardless of the reason, the plays in practice that ended in touchdowns didn't create the same result in the game.

Life is very similar.

You can create any plans you want. No matter how much time you spend planning, reality will inevitably be different.

It doesn't mean you won't be able to achieve your goals.

In fact, the people who achieve their goals in life are experts at dealing with any obstacles that pop up as they pursue their plan. Success eludes those who have never faced obstacles.

The same way that a team can still win the game even though they don't score a touchdown on every play, a resilient and resourceful person can find a way to achieve success in their life.

The sooner that you realize life will throw obstacles in your way, the better you will become at navigating these surprises.

One of my favorite quotes is from the famous boxer Mike Tyson: "Everyone has a plan until they get punched in the face."

This is so true.

Anyone can create a plan, but winners are the ones who achieve success when the plan falls apart.

Dad

True innovators can adapt to any environment.

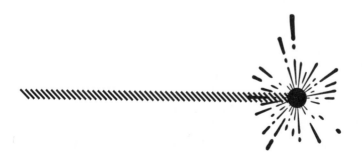

Childhood is not a crutch

Sofia & Leo,

It has become popular for people to use their childhood to explain away the problems in their life today.

There has been an explosion in the frequency of words like trauma, anxiety, and PTSD. (*Example: 'I couldn't score a goal because the coach's criticism gives me PTSD.'*) Many people use their childhoods as a crutch to have a perpetual excuse for their bad behavior or poor results.

While there are certainly horrific situations some kids go through in their childhood that could have a negative impact on them, the vast majority of people I've come across are using this perspective as an excuse. It is the epitome of the victim mindset.

Instead, I think bowhunter Cameron Haines said it best in his book, *Endure*: "It is easy to use your childhood as a crutch instead of seeing it as a chisel."

The situations you encounter throughout your life are molding you into the person you will become. This is how you gain experience. This is how you learn what you like and don't like, along with what to do in various circumstances.

When I was growing up, there were many things I didn't like about my life. My full name felt too proper and old-school, so I told everyone to call me "AJ" instead of "Anthony." I had four brothers so my parents could never take the whole family on an exotic vacation that required us to fly anywhere together. And the most frustrating thing was that my parents refused to ever give my brothers and I an allowance. If I ever wanted to go to the movies or do anything that required spending money, I needed to find a lawn to mow or a snowy driveway to shovel.

Looking back, I am eternally grateful for each of these things today. They helped me morph into the modern version of myself. Everyone calls me Anthony. I now find great pleasure in traveling to various places around the world. And I made a career out of business and investing, so I never had to rely on anyone else for money.

In hindsight, my childhood was incredible. A true chisel.

Don't look for excuses in the rearview mirror. The past created your strength. Use it to your advantage.

Dad

Life is a series of obstacles and tests. Those who learn to be resilient, persistent, and optimistic have the upper hand.

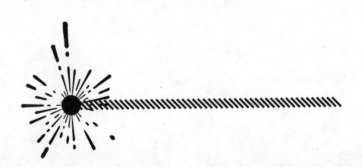

Simplicity signals mastery

Sofia & Leo,

The world is full of people who don't know what they are talking about.

When you run into these people, they will use a few tricks to make it seem like they are smart. They will spend an enormous amount of time using fancy words or complex theories to explain their ideas and opinions.

Tune out the noise. Do not fall for the nonsense.

If someone truly understands something, they should be able to explain it in a simple and concise way.

I learned this lesson when I first learned about bitcoin and cryptocurrencies. There were hundreds of people writing and talking about the new technology. Many of them were using big words and explaining highly-nuanced concepts that I didn't understand.

I was so impressed by them. I wanted to learn from them. Maybe if I read enough books and talked to enough people, I could be like them one day.

But over time I realized that I was wrong.

These people had no clue what they were talking about. To compensate for the lack of true understanding, the individuals would use tactics to sound smart. The truth about the level of their knowledge can be quickly exposed if someone asks enough questions.

Thankfully for me, I had a podcast that allowed me to ask hundreds of questions to an individual. There were many times where someone who I previously thought was smart would be exposed as a good talker who didn't know too much.

This created pattern-recognition for me. I eventually started to be suspicious of anyone who used big words or seemed to make things needlessly complicated.

While the average person may be fooled by these charlatans, I saw this as a tell-tale sign that the person did not know what they were talking about.

You should be aware of the same lesson.

It applies in any field where someone is talking about any subject—from mortgages, to sports, to leadership, to plumbing, to anything else. If someone is waffling, or obscuring things with unnecessary complexity, then they either do not know what they are talking about, or they are trying to trick their audience.

You should learn to communicate in simple, concise language yourself. Don't overcomplicate things. Avoid the fancy words and complex explanations.

Simplicity signals mastery.

Use this knowledge to your advantage. It takes diligence and patience. It's always tempting to write more, give a more detailed explanation, or try to impress people with your knowledge. It's much harder to get a point across concisely and simply.

As French mathematician and philosopher Blaise Pascal wrote: "I have made this [letter] longer than usual because I have not had time to make it shorter."

Do the hard work. Be concise. Use basic words. And prove to everyone you know what you are talking about.

Dad

Smart people use simple language.

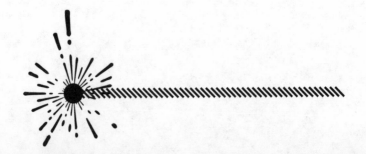

Slow is smooth, smooth is fast

Sofia & Leo,

We live in a world optimized for instant gratification.

You can get almost anything you want with the press of a few buttons on the supercomputer in your pocket. Information will be shown to you in seconds. Food will be delivered in minutes. And packages from Amazon will arrive within hours.

But be very careful—speed does not always produce the best results.

I learned this lesson twice in my life. First, in the military, and then again when building my first asset management firm.

The military lesson was memorable because we could lose our life if we didn't learn this simple concept. While preparing for war, our instructors would spend hours per day teaching us how to enter buildings to search for bad guys.

Hours of preparation for minutes of action.

You get a group of men to line up outside the building, someone opens the door, and then the group tries to enter the building one-by-one to start the search.

Your natural instinct is to enter the building as quickly as possible and run towards the room that the bad guys are located in. The faster you get there, the quicker you can deal with them.

But going fast is actually a horrible idea. Let me explain.

When you run into a building, there are a few things that could go wrong. For example, you could run by someone who is hiding. You could accidentally trigger a trip wire that is attached to a bomb. Or you could create chaos and uncertainty, which confuses your teammates and leads to them accidentally shooting you.

Regardless of the scenario, running quickly into a building is not smart.

Instead, the military trains soldiers to ingrain a mantra in their head: "Slow is smooth, smooth is fast."

The thought process is that soldiers should optimize for cohesion when entering a building, not speed. The more a team can shoot, move, and communicate together, the higher likelihood that the team will accomplish the mission safely.

After weeks of practicing this skill, our team was able to quietly enter a building, search each room methodically, and communicate effectively without talking. Even though we weren't running quickly, the enemy couldn't tell.

We were smooth, so we appeared to be fast.

That lesson always stuck with me because it was counterintuitive. Thankfully, I was ready to put it into practice the next time an opportunity presented itself.

That opportunity happened to surface when I was building my first asset management firm, Morgan Creek Digital. Our team was in the middle of fundraising for a new investment fund. I had been flying across the country multiple times per week looking to speak with any investor who may be interested. In fact, I took approximately 120 flights in 2019.

Why all these flights? Because fundraising wasn't going too well. People said they were interested in what we were doing, but very few investors had been willing to write checks.

Rather than get frustrated, I thought back to the military mantra of "slow is smooth, smooth is fast."

We didn't need to get every single person we spoke with to say yes. Instead, we needed to get a small number of the right people to say yes.

We devised a compelling new strategy that we would execute carefully over time. This was not an overnight-success strategy, but we believed if we focused on the process then we would ultimately be successful.

And that is exactly what happened.

Even though a lot of investors had told us "no," we eventually raised a total of ~$140 million in three years. It had not happened quickly, but the persistence we showed to carry out the strategy prevailed.

Our pitch got better with each meeting. The team became more cohesive. Our investment portfolio started to show investment gains. And we slowly built a compelling process.

Next thing we knew, we popped our heads up and had raised a decent amount of money. What appeared to be fast results to outsiders was really a smooth operation internally. We had focused on what we could control and made sure to avoid rushing to our demise.

Whether it is the military or business, sometimes you have to slow down to go faster.

Slow is smooth, smooth is fast.

Dad

Don't confuse motion with progress.

Never argue with a fool

Sofia and Leo,

I heard a saying years ago that I couldn't forget: "Never argue with a fool because no one can tell who is who from afar."

I have found this to be true throughout my life.

The easiest place to see this phenomenon play out is on the internet. There are millions of people who come together on various websites with different backgrounds, different perspectives, and different mindsets.

Most of the people are looking to learn from one another, but every once in a while you run into a complete fool.

These people are not interested in learning, getting better, or participating in a constructive conversation. They tend to spend their time trolling others. Their goal is to create digital havoc and chaos.

Don't argue with them.

You will not be able to change their mind. Engaging with them will only be a waste of your time. Most important of all, other people looking in from the outside can't tell who is the fool between the two people who are arguing. There are no winners in a game like this.

Another great quote comes from Mark Twain: "Never argue with stupid people, they will drag you down to their level and then beat you with experience." Losing an argument is bad enough, but losing to a stupid fool is even worse.

My experience has been that intelligent, good-natured people don't waste their time arguing on the internet. They are too busy learning or building something of value.

You want to increase the odds that you collide with smart people and decrease the odds that you collide with fools. A great way to do this is to avoid arguing on the internet in general.

Take NBA star LeBron James as an example. He has listened to well-known sports commentator Skip Bayless critique his career for nearly two decades. But LeBron has never responded. Not a single time.

Lebron is above the fray. You should always be too.

Don't argue with a fool.

Dad

Arguing with strangers on the internet is a waste of time.

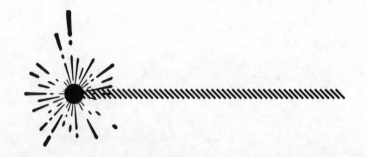

Change your mind when the facts change

Sofia & Leo,

Never be too stubborn to change your mind.

Humans are very good at developing opinions. We look at the available information and create a strong point of view. But you have to be careful—the world is not a static place.

Information is dynamic. The facts change. And when they do, you have to be willing to change your mind.

At the start of 2020, your mother and I were living in New York City. We loved it. There was nothing that could make us ever want to leave the greatest city in the world. Well, that was true until a pandemic struck, New York City shut down, and the local government began to overreach.

The facts had changed, so we changed our mind.

Mom and I moved to the beautiful city of Miami. The weather was amazing. Taxes were low. Many intelligent, hard-working entrepreneurs were flocking to the city at the time. It seemed like paradise.

But after 2.5 years, we realized something was off.

Miami didn't have the same fast-paced environment as New York City, nor did it provide the daily energy that you get when you walk outside your door each morning on an island with millions of people.

We realized that we missed New York. When we told a few of our friends, they thought we were insane. Each friend would rattle off the various reasons why we shouldn't move back—the sunny weather, the low taxes, and the tech ecosystem in Miami was growing.

Maybe they were right. Maybe they weren't. We don't know the future any better than anyone else.

However, we did know that New York City had completely reversed course. The city reopened. The ridiculous government mandates were dropped. And the public health crisis was gone.

New York City was back.

Once again, the facts had changed, so we changed our minds.

Less than three years after we moved to Miami, your mom—who was pregnant with Leo at the time—and I moved back to New York City. Yes, it was burdensome to sell our house and pack it up a year after we had moved in. Yes, it was annoying to answer endless questions from family and friends about the move. Yes, it was difficult to reorganize the entire company when we decided to leave Miami.

But upon returning, it was obvious we had made the right choice when we saw the smile on Sofia's face at the playground. It was worth all the hassle and headaches.

The big takeaway from these two moves is to never be too stubborn to change your mind. Don't worry about what other people will say. Use your critical thinking skills to make the best decision for you even if it doesn't make sense to anyone else.

Many things will change throughout your life. The environment you are in. The people you are around. The information you consume. The things you aspire to accomplish.

Don't get stuck in your ways. Be willing to change your mind.

Dad

Surround yourself with people who are intellectually humble enough to change their mind.

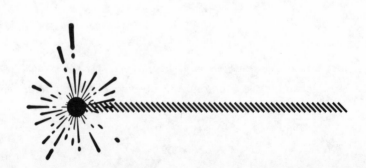

You can't be rational with an irrational person

Sofia & Leo,

Your life will be defined by your ability to communicate with people. Nearly everything you do will be based on effective communication—from talking to your teacher to making new friends to negotiating a big business deal.

It is all about communication.

But I want to offer you a slight nuance: In some rare situations, refusing to communicate is actually the best form of communication.

Let me give you an example from my life.

When I was a young man, I started a business with three friends that I had known for about a decade. We were close, and the idea of starting a business together seemed like the greatest plan ever. It would allow us to hang out more, while also making money together.

Win-win.

The problem was that it quickly became obvious that I had a different expectation of what it would take to succeed. My friends liked the idea of being entrepreneurs, but they didn't actually know what that meant. I would work 12 hour days. They would not.

The difference in our commitment eventually wore on me. We started to disagree more and more. I was willing to do anything to succeed, while they were more interested in making sure everyone was having fun.

As our disagreements became more ridiculous, I grew more frustrated. It was a bad situation that was only getting worse. I didn't know what to do, and given that I was only about 23 years old, I didn't have a lot of experience either.

So I called my dad (your grandfather).

When I told him the situation, he responded with one sentence: "You should get as far away from these guys as you can."

I was shocked. My dad knew my friends. They had come over to our house many times when we were growing up. He would always ask how they were doing. He genuinely cared about them and wanted to see them be successful.

So why was he telling me to get away from them?

My dad explained: "You can't be rational with an irrational person."

His read of the situation was that the four friends had entered into a business with radically different expectations of what they wanted to build and how they wanted to build it.

Given that there was a difference of expectation from the beginning, it would be impossible to change the behavior or commitment of my friends. I was trying to use logic to drive a business outcome. They were using emotion to protect their newfound lifestyle of freedom and fun.

It is very hard to convince someone they are wrong. Usually, they dig their heels in deeper and become more committed to their perspective. From the outside, this doubling-down can be seen as wildly stubborn and increasingly irrational.

My dad's point was not to abandon my friends nor was it to hope they failed. Instead, he was pointing out to me that each side thought the other side was being irrational. Once you reach that point, there is no amount of reasoning that will bridge the gap. There was no way the four of us were ever going to agree about the best way forward.

Instead of wasting weeks, months, and potentially years arguing with my friends, he thought it was best that I went and found something new to work on. In hindsight, my dad was right.

You can't be rational with an irrational person.

It is important that you learn to identify who is rational and who is not. Spend the time and effort to find common ground with the rational ones, but get as far away from irrational people as you can.

Dad

You can't be rational with irrational people.

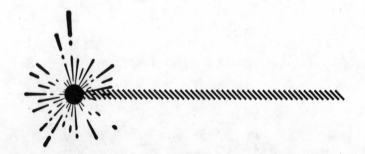

You don't have to win every argument

Sofia and Leo,

Disagreement will happen throughout your life. It could be with a friend, a colleague, or your significant other. Spend enough time with someone and eventually you will find yourself in an argument.

But you don't need to win every argument.

In fact, it can be powerful to intentionally let the other person win. When I was younger, I didn't understand this. I would argue with people for hours. Nothing was held back. It wasn't about finding a solution, but rather, I was obsessed with winning the argument.

I win. They lose. Winning was always my objective.

This is an immature way of looking at close relationships. Life does not have to be zero-sum. It is possible for both of you to win.

Most arguments boil down to different perspectives or different objectives. When you are in this situation, ask yourself, "Is this argument really that important?"

It almost never is.

If you realize that the argument is more petty than important, there is a simple way to move closer to a solution—give the other person a way out of the disagreement without losing face.

Tell them you see where they are coming from. Explain that you are sympathetic to their viewpoint.

Let them keep their respect and dignity. Never try to embarrass them.

Arguments happen. You don't have to win each one. Save your energy for the arguments that actually matter. The rest of them are just distractions from the happy life you are pursuing.

Dad

A true sign of intelligence is understanding that other people may have opinions that differ from yours, but you don't have to attack or berate them over it.

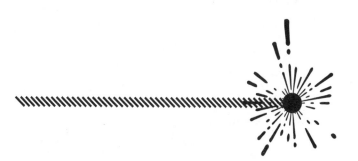

How to be unhappy

Sofia & Leo,

Everyone wants to be happy, but few people know how to achieve this mythical milestone.

It's natural that when people think about how to achieve happiness, they look around at the other people in their lives. What kind of car do they have? What house do they live in? How much money do they make? How do they spend their leisure time? Are they married with kids? Do they seem happy?

This is human nature. You want to understand how you stack up against your friends, family, and colleagues. This is an alluring but dangerous path.

Comparing yourself to other people is an express lane to unhappiness.

You have to remember that every person's situation is different. Just because you may be the same age as someone else, or you may work at the same company, doesn't mean that you should be doing the same things or living the same lives. It makes no sense why two people, who come from different backgrounds and have different goals, would want to make the same decisions.

When I was in college, I took a huge gamble. The majority of the students that I graduated with had goals of becoming a doctor, a lawyer, or a Wall Street financier. It was obvious to me that I would not become a doctor or a lawyer, so it was tempting to spend all my time trying to position myself for a Wall Street job.

These jobs paid well, they were prestigious, and people were usually able to leverage them into great careers. There was just one problem—the idea of wearing a suit and tie to work, while being told what to do by some rich prick, sounded horrible to me.

Even though everyone else wanted one of these jobs, I knew deep down that I would hate it.

The problem was that if I didn't take a Wall Street job, then all my friends would be making much more money than me as soon as we graduated. They would be able to afford nice apartments. Go out to eat multiple times per week. Travel around the world a few times per year. Essentially, they would be living a luxurious life, and I wouldn't.

This really made me think—do I want their future life?

The answer was no.

While most of the people pursuing Wall Street jobs cared about the money, I genuinely only cared about freedom. I didn't want anyone telling me what to do. I didn't want to work 14-hour days on something I didn't care about. And I definitely did not want to be told what clothes to wear.

Thankfully, I had enough self-confidence to refrain from pursuing one of these jobs. Not only did I ultimately have much more success by striking out on my own, but I was also a significantly happier person than my friends on Wall Street.

I had figured out the cheat code to life. I was doing what I wanted to do, regardless of what other people were doing or what material possessions they had. I had freedom.

If I had made the mistake of comparing myself to my peers, then I would have tried to win the game they were playing. I wouldn't have been able to understand that I wasn't interested in winning that game.

I was optimizing for a completely different outcome.

As I achieved certain milestones that mattered to me, such as being able to work from anywhere in the world, the importance of never comparing yourself to someone else became clear.

Remember, comparing yourself to other people is an express lane to unhappiness.

So if you want to be happy, realize that the goal is to play and win your game. As my friend Naval Ravikant says, "The only real test of intelligence is if you get what you want out of life."

Dad

Genuinely caring about what you work on is a big competitive advantage.

Optimize your content diet

Sofia & Leo,

Most people understand the importance of eating well and exercising. People want to live a long, healthy life. They understand that the inputs drive the outcomes. If they were to eat junk food all day and neglect to exercise, their health would deteriorate.

Garbage in, garbage out.

When I met your mother, she taught me how to take this idea a step further. Just as we obsess over the quality of the food we put into our bodies, we should also obsess over the quality of the information that we put into our brains.

She called it a "content diet," explaining that what you eat is who you are, and what you read is who you become.

The idea highlighted the perils of consuming low-quality information. The more you consume trashy reality television, the higher the chance you start emulating those behaviors. The more you read books filled with relationship drama, the more you start to internalize the concept as being normal. The more you watch short clips of your friends at the club every weekend, the more you want to go to the club next weekend.

So I asked your mom to help me implement this idea into my life. She told me that we had to first conduct a content audit.

She had me take an honest look at the content I consumed on a daily basis. What do I read? What do I watch? What do I listen to? Who do I hang out with?

Thankfully, for me, it was almost all business-related content.

There was no reality television, game shows, or fiction books. But I did have one major deficiency—I was spending hours a day consuming information online.

This information could come from an individual posting on social media or from an article outlining the latest development in a news event. Regardless of the format, the important part was that the majority of the information I was consuming was only relevant for a few days. The value of this information was short-lived.

We decided that I should experiment with changing my content diet.

The biggest change I made was to begin reading one physical book per week. The topic was less important than the act of building the habit. Some of the books were about business, while others were about music, health, science, psychology, or history.

The reason this change was important was two-fold: first, the physical book ensured that I wouldn't find myself scrolling endlessly on social media; and second, books are almost always written for consumption over long periods of time, so the content has a longer shelf life.

It was hard to change my content diet at first. I felt like I might miss something in the news. I feared that I would become uninformed. But the exact opposite happened—I became better informed, because I was learning about different subjects. I was learning about history. I was beginning to understand how other industries worked, or how titans of the past built their companies.

The simple idea of improving my content diet put me on a completely different path. I began generating new ideas, having more interesting conversations, and becoming a more informed, well-rounded person.

Most important of all, I started to take insights from different books and apply them to my own life.

Quality in, quality out.

My big takeaway from this exercise was that more money and time should be spent educating people on having a healthy content diet. Most people know the quality of the food we consume matters, but few think about the information we put in our brains.

Now that you know, make sure you are pursuing high-value information. Don't consume trashy television, spend hours per day scrolling on social media, or reading the latest gossip news. Find books, podcasts, TV shows, and social media accounts that will improve your mind.

As your mom says, "Don't let yourself run on autopilot. Be the one to choose what to feed your brain."

Your career, family, and community just may be counting on it.

Dad

People overcomplicate learning. Find smart people and ask them questions. Find good books and read them. Find things you don't know, google them.

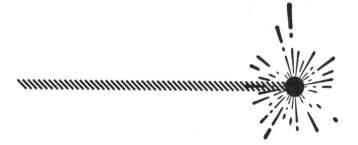

Information is a currency

Sofia & Leo,

Accumulate as much information as you can.

Information runs the world. It is a currency for opportunity. Billy Walters, the best sports gambler in history, said: "The more information you accumulate, the more opportunities you create."

I agree with Billy.

Whether you are evaluating a business deal, negotiating a raise at work, or trying to make the best decision about what restaurant to eat at tonight, your outcome will be improved by having access to more information.

It has always surprised me how few people understand this concept.

Information is how you get informed on a topic. The more informed you are, the better the decision you make.

This is not rocket science.

I was once looking to rent an apartment in New York City with your mother. The building was incredibly nice. The location was perfect. The apartment was available exactly when we wanted to move in.

There was only one problem—the owner was delusional about the cost of rent.

Rather than sit around and complain to the owner, I took a few hours and found as many comparable units as possible. I brought this data to the owner to explain why the apartment would never be rented for the asking price.

Although the owner didn't like it, he was overwhelmed by the data.

The truth hit him in the head. Eventually, we rented the apartment for the price that we had originally suggested. The only way that we could have been successful in that situation was to be more informed than the person with whom we were negotiating. We had to have as much information as possible.

Another time, I was on the opposite end of the situation.

While working at Facebook, one of my bosses held an annual review. He went over my performance for the year, which included driving tens of millions of dollars in revenue for the company.

At the end of the conversation, my boss told me that I would be receiving a $5,000 raise. Since I wasn't expecting to get a raise, I was ecstatic. There were a lot of things that I could do with $5,000 in my mid-20s.

But then something crazy happened a few days later.

One of my colleagues shared that they had received a $20,000 raise during the same annual review. This individual was intelligent and hard-working, but they had not been able to positively impact the business in the same way that I had.

This person had something I didn't have though—he knew how to best negotiate a raise and was able to advocate to their boss that they should get the highest increase in salary possible.

This guy simply had more information than me.

Since that incident, I vowed to be the most informed person in every situation that mattered. Sometimes money was on the line. Other times, I wanted to save time or energy. Information became a currency.

Regardless of the situational details, I try to gather as much information as possible.

You should too.

Dad

Build mental strength by exposing yourself to different ideas, different perspectives, and different belief systems.

Document good ideas

Sofia and Leo,

Ideas run the world.

There are good ideas and bad ideas. Your job is to find as many of the good ideas as you can, and store them in your brain. Good ideas often hide in plain sight.

The big question is how do you find them?

I created a system that seems to have worked well for me. I broke everything down into four areas where I could find a good idea—books, social media, conversations, and audio/video content.

Let's use books as an example. My process starts by reading a physical book and highlighting the best sentences or sections. Once I complete the book, I go back to the beginning and manually transcribe each highlight into a list of notes on my computer.

Once I have transcribed all the highlights, I then use the newly created list as the basis for a set of notes that I write about the book, including the main ideas, my favorite quotes, and my personal takeaways.

This system works well because it requires me to read the best parts of the book multiple times before I am done. I read the content in the book, then I read it a second time while I am highlighting it, then I read it a third time while I am transcribing it, and then I read it when I am writing up my notes. That is at least four times I have read and thought about the most important ideas.

It is hard to forget something profound and useful after you have read it four times.

Like so much of the advice in this book, this seems simple—and it is!—but it works. Most people don't take the time to do it. How much more time does it take to read a book and write up notes as I described here, than it does to read the book just once? It's an extra investment of time and effort. Most people may not want to put in the work, or they may not believe how effective something so simple can be.

Another good example is conversations. I have been fortunate to meet many interesting people in my life. Some are very famous, some are very wealthy, some are completely unknown, and some have not been successful at all. I make it a goal to learn something from each one of them.

In order to remember what I learn from these conversations, I always take a few minutes after a meeting or phone call to write down whatever I remember. If I still remember the idea by the time the conversation is over, then it must have been important, high-quality, or both.

There are a number of academic studies that suggest our memory improves when we write things down. I am not sure if that works for everyone, but it works wonders for me.

As you go through life, you will meet lots of people as well. Don't be afraid to ask them questions about their life, their profession, or what they have learned over the years. People love to talk about themselves and you will be surprised how often successful people are excited about telling you important ideas.

The key is to figure out a system to document all these ideas. If you don't create a system, then you will forget most of the things that you learn. Our brains can only handle so much.

Take a few minutes each day to write down what you have learned. Your future self will thank you.

Dad

The world seems to separate itself into two groups—the people who never stop learning and everyone else.

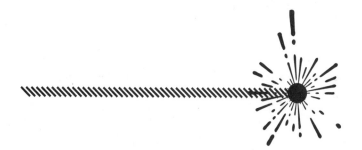

Spend less than you make

Sofia & Leo,

Money runs the world. If you learn to master it, then you will be free forever.

You will meet people at every stage of life who have trouble with money. Nearly all of them will say they don't make enough of it. They will complain about their income problem.

But this is almost never the true problem.

The root of the issue is that the majority of people with money problems have a spending problem. They spend more than they make. These people tend to rely on credit cards and loans to finance their lifestyle.

I'll give you two examples of the different approaches someone can take.

Your mother's annual salary was about $35,000 when she moved to New York City in 2014. After she paid her taxes, bills, transportation, and rent, she only had a fraction of that to live on. This means she had to survive in New York City, one of the most expensive cities in the world, on the $108 per week that she had budgeted for discretionary spending.

Rather than live above her means, your mom would keep a list of expenses each week. If she got a $26 taxi ride, she wrote it down on the list. A $7 meal from McDonald's? Wrote it down. If she purchased a bottle of water at the corner store for less than $2, she wrote that down too.

No expense was too small.

Thankfully, mom's obsession with the details helped her make it work. Eventually she got a new job with higher pay, but because she had been disciplined, mom never went into debt.

Compare this with the approach of a young technology entrepreneur that I met when we lived in Miami. This man thought that investors would only want to invest in his company if he appeared wealthy. Rather than live within his means, the entrepreneur built a life of wealth fueled by debt.

This wasn't true wealth—this was a mirage.

His Ferrari was leased. The boat that he posted on social media each weekend was leased as well. I found out over time that his credit cards were maxed out and he was always late on his apartment rent payments.

This entrepreneur was taking the opposite approach of your mother.

Eventually, the man couldn't keep up with all the payments he had to make each month. One by one, the bank began to take back his assets. First, it was his boat, but eventually he was left with no car and apartment too.

The last I heard of him, the entrepreneur had to move home to live with his parents after filing personal bankruptcy.

If I was to talk with this young man today, I would ask him, "Was it worth it?" He had created an image of a life that he had not yet earned. The desire for social acceptance overwhelmed his common sense. And he committed the ultimate financial sin—living outside his means.

Never spend more money than you make.

Stay on top of the details. Don't lose your discipline. As long as you live within your means, you have a chance to build a life of wealth and freedom.

Dad

The biggest mistake
I see people make
when it comes to
personal finance is
that they spend more
money than they
make.

Simple rule. Incredibly
hard to execute for
most.

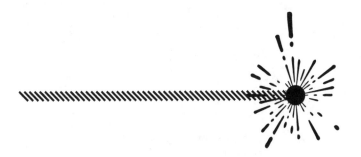

Rich people sell too early

Sofia & Leo,

Investing is hard. It may be one of the hardest things to do consistently well over long periods of time.

One small part of this is that when things do go well, you have to remember to sell.

This may seem like odd advice, so let me explain.

There are tens of thousands of stocks, bonds, currencies, and commodities for you to invest in. The investable universe is so large it could just as well be infinite. But regardless of how much research you do and which investments you choose, the same outcome has remained true throughout history—some of your investments will go up in value and some of them will go down.

That is normal. Don't sweat it.

But if you want to build wealth, you have to remember to sell some of the assets that go up in value.

There is an old saying about this that is worth repeating to yourself periodically: "All my rich friends sold too early."

When things are going well with an investment, you start believing it is only going to go higher and higher and higher. You start to congratulate yourself on finding the investment that is going to change your life and make you rich. Suddenly, you feel like the smartest person in the room. This is human nature.

Be careful. This is a mistake, and it's a mistake I have made myself more times than I wish to admit.

Some investments that go up in value must also come down in value. They can lose value for many different reasons. Sometimes the reasons are obvious, but many times they are not.

It doesn't matter.

What does matter is that you can't count the win until you sell. If you don't get more dollars in your bank account, it doesn't matter what happened to the investment in the meantime.

Selling is more important than most people realize. Too much attention is paid to the "investing" part and not enough to the "selling" part.

Why could this be?

A major reason is that people get scared of a situation where they sell their investment and it then continues to appreciate in value. They feel like this means they have screwed up. It isn't good enough in their eyes to make a profit if they aren't able to make the full profit that would have been possible.

Don't fall into this trap. It is greed talking.

Investing is all about risking capital to capture a return. *Capture* is the key word in that sentence. And the only way to capture a return is to sell an asset once it has appreciated.

You don't have to sell it all at once. You can sell one small piece at a time.

Most of the time when you sell an investment, it will continue to appreciate in price for some period of time. That is okay. Leave some profits for the next person.

The goal isn't to time the top of a market for an asset and get the maximum possible profit every time. The goal is to capture a return. And you have to sell to get the return.

Remember, all my rich friends sold too early.

Join the rich friends. Sell when you have profits. Your bank account will thank you in the future.

Dad

Never count your profits until the money hits the bank.

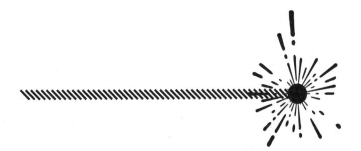

Buy great assets and hold them forever

Sofia & Leo,

Warren Buffett is one of the greatest investors in history. He is famous for saying, "Our favorite holding period is forever."

This is one of the most important financial lessons I can teach you.

Let me explain.

There are very few assets or companies that can withstand the test of time. If you go back 50 years and look at the top companies in the world, that list looks very different from today. Upstart companies innovate to create something new. Innovation leads to disruption of incumbents who are asleep at the wheel. The old companies die and the new companies replace them.

Just as the circle of life dominates the natural world around us, there is a circle of life to assets and companies too.

This is essential to understand as an investor. There will be times when you want to buy an asset, have it appreciate in price, and then sell it for a profit.

Other times, though, you want to buy a great asset and hold it forever.

This second situation is where life-changing returns can be generated.

There are two factors that you are looking for in these potential opportunities: (1) assets that have a high compound annual growth rate; and (2) assets that have a moat which will make it hard for anyone to disrupt them in the future.

For me, the asset that fits this criteria is bitcoin.

The digital currency had a compound annual growth rate of over 100% when I began buying it in 2017. It was also obvious to me that it would be nearly impossible for someone to create a better digital currency (for a host of reasons that took months for me to understand).

Once I understood though, I went all in and bought as much bitcoin as I could. The plan? Hold the bitcoin forever and pass it on to my kids, and then my grandkids, and so on.

It may sound weird to apply Warren Buffett's advice to bitcoin, especially since he has been an outspoken critic of the asset, but his framework worked perfectly for me.

Your goal should be to invest in one or two assets like this in your lifetime. By definition, there can't be a lot of rare assets that can withstand the test of time. Once you do the work and become convinced that an asset fits this criteria, the challenge becomes holding the asset regardless of what happens.

A man named Bill Miller was an investor in Amazon in the late 1990s. When the dotcom crash of 2000 happened, most investors sold as many tech stocks as they could. Bill did the opposite. He tried to buy as much Amazon stock as possible.

Eventually, Bill became the single largest individual shareholder of Amazon outside of Amazon founder Jeff Bezos. As the company recovered from the crash, Bill kept holding his Amazon stock and it turned into one of the best investments, by anyone, in the last 50 years.

Take a page out of Bill and Warren's playbook. Find great assets. Hold them forever. That is how you generate true wealth and gain financial freedom.

Dad

The best investors in the world are really good at doing nothing for long periods of time.

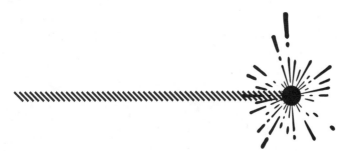

Pictures are memories frozen in time

Sofia & Leo,

Take pictures as often as possible.

You can do this when you meet new people. When you are hanging out with old friends. Whenever you travel to a new place. Or if something happens in your life that is important.

Each picture you capture is a memory written in stone.

You may not look at the photos all the time. In fact, you may never look at the photos. You will forget that you have taken most of them. But on a random day long in the future, you will remember you have the photos and you will look through them.

These photos will trigger memories of fun times, good friends, and cool places you visited. You won't be able to resist smiling as you look through everything you were able to capture.

Taking pictures is one of the activities that I've done in my life that I am most grateful for as I have gotten older.

I have photos from when I was a young kid. There is documentation of various sports achievements, high school friends, or fun parties that we attended. Some of these photos are embarrassing to look at now (I have never claimed to have a good sense for fashion!), but every one of them helps me remember different aspects of my life that made me happy at one point.

I even have a photo from the first day that I met your mother. After meeting her for coffee in the morning, I had convinced her to meet me for dinner that night. Two dates on the first day we knew each other—no one ever accused me of being too patient.

The photo we have together is at a bar after dinner. There are two other people in the photo. I don't even remember their names anymore, but that doesn't matter. You can see the excitement your mom and I had for this new relationship.

It is pretty cool.

I also have photos from my time in the military, including things that were cool and things that were dangerous. I have photos from college, both as a student and as a member of the football team. To be honest, the best college photos are probably from the parties. We threw the best parties!

And I have photos from life as an adult. There is a photo of my co-founders and I starting our first business. I have photos from my time at Facebook. And I have hundreds of photos from various trips I have taken over the years, including India, Israel, Nigeria, Colombia, Iceland, Puerto Rico, Singapore, Mexico, Ireland,

Spain, Italy, the Bahamas, Canada, Indonesia, Bulgaria, Greece, Iraq, Kuwait, and the UK to name a few.

The reason I can even name half of the places that I have visited is because of the photos I took.

But there's one big caveat to this advice: You and I grew up in different eras. When I was little, taking photos was reserved for special occasions—birthdays, trips, and celebrations. Now, everyone has a camera in their pocket. You can take hundreds of photos *a day*.

Make sure you take the time to look at them often.

The human brain is a magnificent machine, but our memories are not perfect. Photos prevent us from forgetting the amazing experiences and people we have the good fortune to come across during our lifetime.

Take photos often. Your older self will thank you. And, as a bonus, your photos will be a gift to future generations who want to know who you were as well.

Dad

Life is about memories.

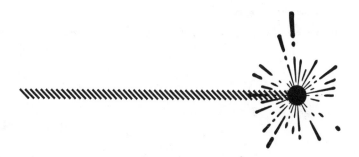

Weird things can change the world

Sofia & Leo,

Many of the greatest ideas sounded bizarre at first.

Airbnb started off with the founders renting air mattresses on their kitchen floor. Facebook started off as a website to find attractive people on Harvard's campus. The internet started as a network for nerds to communicate with each other. The idea of humans being able to fly like birds in an airplane seemed outlandish, and the theory of the Earth revolving around the Sun was intensely rejected at first.

An important truth is that weird things can evolve to change the world.

I have seen this pattern repeat throughout my life. A great example is bitcoin. I first heard about the digital currency in the early 2010s. The idea of money which could not be controlled by a government seemed insane.

Only criminals and anti-government people would want to use it, right?

Man, was I wrong on that one. Bitcoin grew from a little-known idea to one of the biggest stories in financial markets. It was eventually worth trillions of dollars and held by most of the best investors in the world.

To this day, no one knows who created it. There has been nothing like it prior to its invention. The idea was weird. The early adopters were weird. The nomenclature was weird. Everything about bitcoin was weird.

But that didn't prevent bitcoin from succeeding.

In fact, you could argue that bitcoin succeeded *because* it was weird. It had been constructed in a way that was in opposition of every other currency in the world. This contrarian approach ended up being right. It became a consensus idea about 15 years after it was launched.

Weird things can change the world.

In other words, you must never be scared to do weird things. If you have a weird idea, pursue it. If you are interested in something weird, spend more time learning about it. If you have a weird friend, spend more time with them to understand their perspective on the world.

Most people run away from weird things, but I have found in my life that great value can be created by running toward them instead.

It is not easy to do it in the moment. Your friends may judge you for it. You may feel like you will have a hard time succeeding on the traditional path in life if you pursue a weird idea.

Don't worry about what anyone else thinks. The most extraordinary things grew out of something odd. Rarely will the cool, popular, shiny thing change the world. Follow your interests even if others label them as weird.

Dad

Independent thinking is the root of all good decisions.

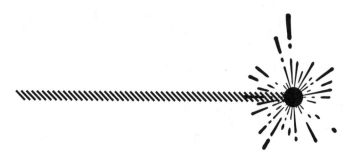

You can't live an extraordinary life sitting on your couch

Sofia and Leo,

You can't understand the world if you never see it.

Traveling is the best education you will ever receive. It will immerse you in another culture. It will show you how other people live day-to-day. And it will give you a greater appreciation for your own opportunities and privileges.

Every single time I have traveled somewhere, I have come back more educated and inspired.

For example, I took a two-week trip to Nigeria in 2017. This wasn't your average trip though. Rather than stay on Victoria Island, which is where most of the American tourists stay, my friend and I rented a hotel room about a mile from Computer Village in Lagos. This is the heart of the largest city in the country.

During the trip, I felt like I was being simultaneously thrust into the future and the past.

On one hand, Nigeria was still a developing nation with a need for better infrastructure, safety, and economic opportunity. It was difficult to see the level of poverty that some Nigerians had to endure. Basic needs were unmet and plenty of people seemed to have lost hope.

On the other hand, the population was incredibly young and the total number of citizens is growing so fast that it is estimated there will be more Nigerians than Americans by 2050. It is also one of the highest-ranking developing nations when it comes to adoption of the internet and smartphones. I felt as though I was getting a sneak peek into the future.

But things took a turn during the middle of our trip.

My friend and I were in an Uber. A police officer was conducting a traffic checkpoint, and they asked our driver to pull over to the side of the road. Within a few minutes, the officer asked my friend and I to step out of the vehicle.

Rather than ask us questions about who we were or where we were going, the police officer simply told us to give him the money in our wallets. It was shocking. That would never happen in the United States.

But thankfully, we had been warned about this possibility. My cash was sitting comfortably under the driver's seat and my friend's money was tucked into his socks. We just smiled and kept telling the officer that we had no money on us.

Eventually, either because we were too stubborn or too annoying, the officer decided to let us go. At no point did we feel unsafe, nor did we ever feel like we were in danger. We saw the situation for what it was—a different reality than the one we were used to in America.

I often think back to that experience as a perfect example of why I love to travel.

You can't live an extraordinary life sitting on your couch. There is a lot to be learned from books and conversations, but nothing will ever replace the real-life experience of immersing yourself into another culture.

Make sure you find the time to travel. It can be to another city, another state, or halfway around the world. Get out there and live. Avoid the tourist traps. Eat with the locals. Ask them about the best things to do on weekends. Don't follow the herd. Find the unique experiences.

I'll leave you with the words of the late renegade chef Anthony Bourdain: "Travel isn't always pretty. It isn't always comfortable. Sometimes it hurts, it even breaks your heart. But that's OK. The journey changes you; it should change you. It leaves marks on your memory, on your consciousness, on your heart, and on your body. You take something with you. Hopefully, you leave something good behind."

Dad

You can improve your instincts by exposing yourself to many different people and situations.

Each new experience gives you a feedback loop that allows you to improve your instincts algorithm over time.

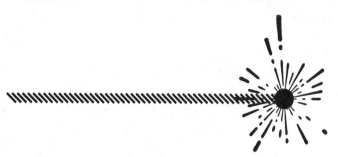

Live your life as a documentary

Sofia and Leo,

You will live an extraordinary life if you pretend you are creating a documentary of your days.

Think about the documentaries or movies that you love. None of them are boring. No one wants to watch a film about a mundane life. They need adventure, achievement, creative problem-solving, and excitement.

You will live your life this way if you constantly think about making a great film.

Before you were born, your mother asked if I wanted to run the New York City marathon. I told her, "No." I had lived in New York for years and told myself that I didn't need to run a marathon to see more of the city.

The truth is that I simply didn't want to run a marathon. Just thinking about running 26.2 miles made my knees hurt. But your mother knows me too well.

She came back to me a week later and said, "What if we run the original marathon in Greece?"

That question caught my attention. She explained that this race was the same path that Athenian messenger Pheidippides ran nearly 2,500 years ago when he brought news of victory from the battlefield of Marathon to Athens.

As soon as I heard that, I knew I had to do it. The epic story of running the original marathon course would be well worth the short-term pain of running 26.2 miles.

A few months later, we flew to Greece. We ran the marathon. It was terrible. There were hills and the sun was beating down on us relentlessly. Your mom even cried.

But we finished the authentic Athens Marathon.

It took us from Marathon, Greece to the Olympic Stadium in Athens, which is the birthplace of the modern Olympic Games. Not only did we conquer the same historic steps that Pheidippides had taken thousands of years before, but we left with an epic experience that we could re-tell hundreds of times in the years to come. As you can see, I am even re-telling the story now.

This is what it means to live your life as if you are creating a documentary.

It is easy to get caught up in the mundane, repetitive nature of your day-to-day schedule. You have to fight this entropy. No one wants to watch a boring biopic. Do epic things. Pursue adventure, action, and excitement.

Create memories that give you stories to tell to others in the future.

Dad

Don't spend so much time over-optimizing your life that you forget to enjoy it.

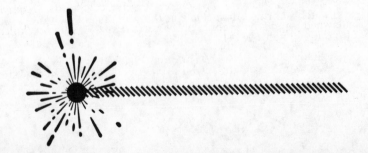

We are all going to die

Sofia & Leo,

We are all going to die.

I learned this lesson at 20 years old, and it transformed my life. I was a young soldier deployed in Iraq just north of Baghdad. Our military unit was attacked one day, a few hours after midnight while out on patrol.

Chaos broke out. Bombs. Gunshots. Tanks. Helicopters.

It was straight out of a movie.

When the dust settled, the enemy had killed one of our soldiers. We had wounded and captured one of theirs.

I will never forget the feeling driving back to our base afterward. I was in shock. I was sad. I was angry. And I was thankful—it quickly dawned on me that I could have been the soldier who was killed.

My life has never been the same after that day.

I had come to the realization that every human's life ends at the same place: death.

It was only once I understood that we all die that I could really start living. Famed philosopher Marcus Aurelius wrote, "It is not death that a man should fear, but he should fear never beginning to live."

That is how I felt, so I took my new outlook on life and started living in a blaze of glory. I began taking things seriously. I started investing in my close relationships. I traveled more. I sought out incredible experiences.

Whatever I could think of that would help me enjoy the short period of time we get on Earth, I pursued passionately.

You should do the same thing.

The metal bracelet with the soldier's name engraved on it that I wear on my right wrist is a daily reminder to live life. It sounds cliche, but everything could end in an instant. Make sure you enjoy your time before that day comes.

When you are young, it is easy to think you will live forever. Let's be honest—30, 40 or 50 years really does feel like forever.

But time passes quickly. One day you are a teenager with little responsibility and a lot of ambition. The next you are a middle-aged adult with kids, lots of responsibility, and a low appetite for risk.

The sooner you understand this evolution that everyone goes through, the faster you can start squeezing as much enjoyment out of life.

We all die.

It may sound morbid, but it is the truth. Come to terms with it so you can start living.

Dad

You are going to die—we each get a finite amount of time on this earth so do something bold, courageous, and ambitious.

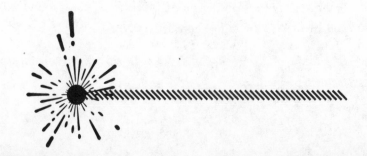

Walk outside daily

Sofia & Leo,

A walk has never seen a problem it didn't like.

Every time that I am faced with an issue that I can't figure out, I go for a walk outside. It could be a challenge at work. Maybe a relationship that is fraying and I don't know how to handle it. Or I could simply be in search of a new idea.

A long walk never fails to cure the issue.

Before you roll your eyes, understand that it is scientifically proven that walking outside helps generate ideas. One part of the science is that walking increases your heart rate, which means more blood will flow to your brain. Another part is a slew of new brain cell connections that are activated when walking. And, lastly, your brain is hardwired to work on problems in the background while you are focused on doing a rote activity like walking.

Regardless of the reason, get outside and walk when you are facing a problem.

This secret has been known for centuries by many successful entrepreneurs, investors, and thinkers. Some of the most famous people who had a habit of walking include Charles Darwin, Albert Einstein, Ludwig Van Beethoven, Aristotle, Socrates, Immanuel Kant, Friedrich Nietzsche, William Wordsworth, Henry David Thoreau, and Virginia Woolf.

Not a bad group to emulate.

My favorite place to walk and think is in New York City's Central Park. There is something special about being surrounded by the chaos of one of the biggest cities in the world but ignoring all of it to spend time alone in your head.

As I go through the park, I see people from different walks of life.

There are horse carriages carrying tourists through the city. Couples enjoying a picnic on the grass. Children running and laughing. A local musician playing his favorite song to passersby who don't seem to notice. Police officers joking with each other as they wait for their shift to end. And food trucks hoping to serve one more pretzel and soda before they go home for the night.

All this stimulus serves a purpose for my brain. It keeps my mind in overdrive. Ideas are firing every few seconds. Some are good, but most are garbage. The point isn't to have as many great ideas as possible, but rather to find the one idea that solves my current problem.

This is why I started to invite other people on these walks with me.

Usually, your mother is walking next to me. She is my favorite walking partner. We discuss whatever problem I am dealing with. Two brains working in overdrive to brainstorm a solution is better than one. As ideas come to us, we verbalize them to each other.

No idea is stupid. It may not be the solution to the problem, but her idea could spark a winning idea in my brain. The opposite is true too.

Walking. Talking. Thinking outside.

This is the formula I have used over and over again to think of creative ways to solve whatever problem I was facing. Many of the world's smartest people have been doing this for thousands of years as well.

Remember, a walk is always a good idea.

Dad

There are few things more enjoyable than a long walk outside with your family.

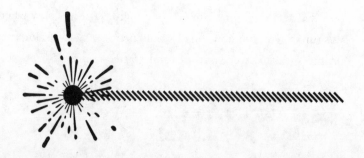

No stress can withstand a proper workout

Sofia and Leo,

Make sure you exercise every single day.

This will transform your good days into great days and your bad days into good days. Working out is one of the only things in your life that has all upside and no downside.

When I was building my first business, I found that I was often stressed out. It became hard to sleep at night because my mind would be racing about my endless to-do list.

A rabid mind is the enemy of sleep.

So I decided to go for a run late one night. I didn't know where I was running to, nor how long I would be running for. I simply put on my sneakers, went outside, and started running through my neighborhood.

I had no headphones on. I didn't have my cell phone with me.

Nothing but me and my thoughts.

As I was running, I noticed that my mind started to wander aimlessly. I started ruminating on unfinished tasks and unsolved problems.

But then something odd started to happen. The more I ran, the more my mind began generating ideas. I thought of some creative solutions to the problems I was facing, and the tasks on my to-do list no longer felt insurmountable. The more I ran, the more mental clarity I received.

This is when I realized an important lesson in life—no stress can withstand a proper workout.

The type of workout doesn't matter. You can go for a run, do a half-hour of yoga, or lift heavy weights until exhaustion. The details matter less than the action of moving your body for a period of time.

Scientists will tell you that exercise releases endorphins and other hormones that improve your mood. Doctors will tell you that exercise reduces your blood pressure and keeps your body healthy. Psychologists will tell you that working out boosts creativity and mental energy.

They are all right.

Working out is important for many different reasons. The beauty is that you don't have to understand them all in order to reap the benefits.

Make sure you move your body every day. You will be happier, healthier, and more productive.

Dad

**Exercise is
mental training
masquerading as
physical training.**

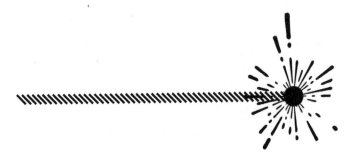

Attack the day

Sofia & Leo,

You must attack the day ferociously.

I do two things every morning when I wake up. First, I look in the mirror and smile. Second, I say to myself, "Today is going to be a great day."

This has been my routine every day for years. I never miss a day. Ever.

You should practice these two actions too.

There is a mountain of research that suggests we can change our mental state by our actions and words. Don't believe me? Try it right now.

Stop reading and smile for one full minute.

I would be shocked if you didn't find yourself in a more cheerful, happy mood. I can't explain why it happens, but I know it is true from personal experience. The smile forces your brain and mood to improve.

The same thing is true for telling yourself that you will have a great day. It sets the tone for the next 24 hours. You can speak reality into existence.

Think about how much more powerful it is to start each day in a good mood than a bad one.

Why would anyone want to start the day pissed off about something that happened yesterday, or worked up about something they read online while scrolling on their phone when they woke up?

Don't do it. Don't give your mind the opportunity to start the day on a bad note.

Now, you may be saying to yourself that smiling and saying the day will be positive is pretty simple, and it is, but there is something else that I have learned from this practice over the years.

The discipline of doing this every morning creates intentionality in your actions. You took a moment to remember to smile. You spent a few seconds to say out loud that you will have a good day.

Those small investments may not seem like a big deal, but they show that you are focused on preparing yourself for success. As I have mentioned, I don't believe in luck. It isn't real. But you can increase the probability that you will accomplish the day's tasks by starting it with a positive mood.

Smile every morning. Remind yourself that you are going to have a great day.

You will notice a difference. I promise.

Dad

Got in an elevator this morning. One guy inside. He has a massive smile, cracks a stupid weather joke, and lets out a deep belly laugh. There is something special about people who simply enjoy life.

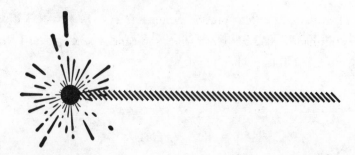

Sleep is nature's doctor

Sofia & Leo,

Prioritize your sleep.

Sleep is nature's doctor. It magically helps your body heal. It gives you more energy to tackle tomorrow. Sleep will make your skin look better, while keeping your body younger. Sleep can save your life.

It is really that important.

I have to admit—it took me almost three decades to figure out this life truth. For the first 30 years of my life, I never prioritized sleep. I would stay up late at night and wake up early in the morning. The goal was to get between four and six hours of rest.

I thought anything more than that was a waste of time.

This flawed thought process dominated everything that I did. I even had a quick response when someone would suggest I sleep more—"I'll sleep when I'm dead."

That isn't true though. It doesn't take a rocket scientist to realize that I was being dumb and naive.

So how did I change my mind?

When the pandemic of 2020 hit the United States, we were all locked inside our homes. I couldn't go out late at night. I didn't have to be up early in the morning to rush off to work the next day. Frankly, it was boring, and there was more free time available than I had experienced in years.

I used that free time to sleep more. I went to bed earlier. I woke up later. I began tinkering with my bedtime routine. What temperature should the room be? Did drinking alcohol before bed help or hurt my sleep quality? What if I drank chamomile tea? How long before bed should I eat or work out?

I didn't know the answers to any of these questions, but I eventually figured them out.

And then something magical started to happen. The more I slept, the healthier I became, the more energy I had, the better mood I was in each day, the less junk food I craved. Most importantly, I was more productive every day.

By increasing the hours and quality of my sleep, nature was doing its job—it was healing my body, allowing me to recharge, and creating an optimal balance of hormones across my body and brain.

After sleeping eight hours a night, I felt unstoppable.

This experience is precisely why I prioritize my sleep to this day. Once you realize how important sleep is, you never go back. You become addicted to the feeling after a great night of sleep. There is nothing in this world like it. No drugs, alcohol, or prescription medicine can beat it.

Sleep is nature's doctor. Make sure you go see the doctor every night.

Dad

The secrets to higher quality sleep:

- Increase your physical activity.

- Make sure you're tired every day.

- Don't eat before bed.

- Limit alcohol.

- Avoid sugar.

- Make your room or bed cold.

- Set an alarm to go to sleep earlier.

Easy rules. Takes discipline to follow.

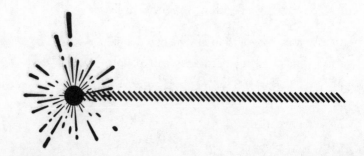

Your intuition is your algorithm

Sofia & Leo,

It is important to trust your intuition.

These gut feelings may seem random or unscientific, but they are actually one of the highest signal pieces of information you can have when making a decision.

You can think of humans like computers—we have hardware and software. By taking care of our bodies, we are constantly improving our hardware and creating resilience for whatever the world throws at us.

At the same time, our software is being updated constantly based on the information we consume, the experiences we endure, and the feedback we receive from the world. We are training our decision-making algorithm as we live our lives.

An easy way to understand this is that people with more experience usually make better decisions than people with no experience.

Not always, but usually. They have seen more and been fortunate enough to see how various decisions and situations play out.

When I was younger, I was always cautious about trusting my intuition. I wanted to gather as much information as possible. I would over-analyze situations. If there was a big decision to make, I would create long pro and con lists. In some way, I was procrastinating instead of making the decision because I didn't have the confidence to trust my intuition.

But then something interesting started to happen. I realized that the good decisions I made were in-line with my initial intuition and the bad decisions happened when I overrode my intuition.

This helped me build the confidence to trust my gut.

My intuition may have saved my life actually. I traveled to India in 2016 with my brother. We spent two weeks traveling the beautiful country and visited five different cities. It was an amazing trip, but there was one dangerous situation that almost derailed it.

On New Year's Eve, as we headed into 2017, my brother and I were on the beach in Goa. We had spent the night celebrating at the W Hotel with some business friends. As we were leaving the party, one of the guests invited us to another party at an adjacent hotel on the beach.

As we approached the entrance, the doormen waved our friends into the party, but they stopped me and my brother. When we asked why we were not allowed in the party, the doormen became much more aggressive. One of them even said, "This is Goa. We make Americans like you disappear here."

That was all we needed to hear. Our collective intuition was telling us that the situation was going to get bad, fast. So my brother and I immediately left and began walking down the beach.

Something seemed off though—our internal algorithms kept telling us we weren't out of trouble yet. It felt like someone was following us, although we couldn't see anyone behind us in the night.

Regardless, we sped up our pace and found an area where we could run over the berm and quietly hide and wait. Sure enough, a few minutes later a group of young men on four-wheelers and bikes came down the beach looking for us.

There have been very few times in my life that I have been scared, but this situation was definitely one of them. My brother and I were halfway across the world in a foreign country with no cell phone service and now there was a group of men who appeared to be looking for us.

Thankfully, we were able to stay put in our hiding spot for a few hours until the sun came up. We returned to the W hotel, retrieved our rental car, and left the area. Who knows what would have happened if we hadn't trusted our intuition that night.

Humans have evolved over 200,000 years and being able to sense danger is a key part of our intuition.

Don't be arrogant enough to believe you are smarter than evolution. Trust your gut. It can be used to make good decisions in business and relationships, but it also may save your life one day.

Dad

Believe in yourself and trust your instincts.

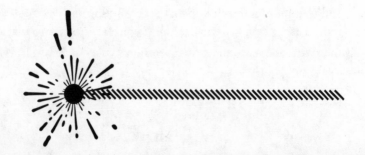

Write letters

Sofia & Leo,

To conclude this collection of letters, I want to write one final letter to you telling you about the value of writing your own letters.

You should write letters as often as you can.

You can use me as the perfect example of this lesson. I despised writing before I met your mom. It reminded me of school, and I didn't think I was very good at it.

But your mom knows best. She pushed me to write more often. An easy prompt she would give me is to pick a person and then write a letter to them about a specific topic. Surprisingly, it became much easier to write when I had a person in mind.

This book contains 65 letters that I have written to you— my children.

I have spent years writing these letters. Each one required me to learn a life lesson, internalize the importance of the lesson, and then write a letter to the next generation so they can learn from my successes *and* my missteps.

The process has been time-consuming, but if you learn even one thing from these letters, then the effort will have been worth it.

But here's the great irony of this book: Even though I thought I wrote it for you, it was me who needed it the most.

Writing each letter forced me to think critically about the lessons I have learned. A letter can't be written in a sloppy way, or the idea is not transferred from the writer to the reader.

Clear writing leads to clear thinking.

So whether or not you enjoy writing, make sure you write letters throughout your life. Write a letter to your mom for her birthday, and tell her what you most appreciate about our family. Write a letter to your best friend, and share some funny stories you hope they'll remember in the years to come. Finally—and most importantly—write a letter to your future self, describing your ambitions, hopes, and desires.

Letters serve as time capsules for all that you have learned and all that you have yet to learn.

Don't waste time. Start today.

Dad

Letters serve as time capsules for all that you have learned and all that you have yet to learn.